The Sinister Serials of
Boris Karloff, Bela Lugosi
and Lon Chaney, Jr.

The Sinister Serials of Boris Karloff, Bela Lugosi and Lon Chaney, Jr.

by Leonard J. Kohl

With the participation of
George E. Turner and Michael H. Price

Midnight Marquee Press, Inc.
Baltimore, Maryland

Cover Design: Susan Svehla

ISBN 1-887664-31-9
Library of Congress Catalog Card Number 99-76001
Manufactured in the United States of America
Printed by Kirby Lithographic Company, Arlington, VA
First Printing by Midnight Marquee Press, Inc., March 2000

Acknowledgments: John Antosiewicz Photo Archives, Betty Cavanaugh, Photofest, Michael H. Price, Wayne Shipley, Linda J. Walter

TABLE OF CONTENTS

Sinister Serials

A TRIBUTE TO
GEORGE E. TURNER

The very day I sent a near-final typescript of this book to the publishers was the day I learned my friend and mentor, George E. Turner, had passed away only shortly before, on Father's Day 1999. It was something of a shock—bad news to all the friends and colleagues whom George had influenced, in so many ways. He inspired a great many writers. He became good friends with many of them: With Michael H. Price, George sustained a "film archaeology" partnership that not only spanned more than three decades, but also continues via works-in-progress that Mike now keeps vital. The Turner orbit would grow to include Wayne Schutz, Jan Alan Henderson, Gary Don Rhodes, Ron Magid, Steve Vertlieb and Roy Kinnard, among others. Some had known George for many years, others only for a brief visit or two, but he treated the lot of us as friends, and we felt the same way about him.

My friend Bill Naras produced a 60th anniversary theatrical tribute to *King Kong* in Chicago, back in 1993. George, as an expert on the Eighth Wonder of the World, was one of our guests, along with Steve Vertlieb, another *Kong* historian. We had hoped that special-effects cinematographer Linwood P. Dunn—who was among George's own mentors—would attend, but he had to cancel about three weeks before the show. He told Bill Naras that the show would be run just as smoothly with George at the helm. Of course, we were disappointed that Mr. Dunn couldn't be with us—after all, he had worked on *King Kong*—but we had a wonderful show, and George did everything he could to make it a success. A friendship formed among all of us, and I kept in touch constantly with George as I wrote articles for *Filmfax* magazine and delved into other projects, one of which evolved into this book. George was constantly helping me whip this manuscript into shape, and I am grateful that he saw one of the later drafts of it. The fact that he meticulously corrected various points and made suggestions throughout the manuscript makes it all the better.

George E. Turner and Steve Vertlieb at the *King Kong* tribute.

George was not only a writer; he was also a cartoonist and worked in special effects and storyboarding for film and television. The author and co-author of numerous books, he also spent a decade as editor of *American Cinematographer*, one of the pre-eminent magazines in the film trade. George was a champion of films from past to present, and was involved in several restorations as a technical consultant. To say that George will be missed is an understatement. I had thought of dedicating this book to him, but I knew he would be embarrassed by such a gesture. I will do so now, however. Thanks, George!

In their best acting, Bela Lugosi, Boris Karloff and Lon Chaney, Jr. created characters who were full of zest, full of gusto—characters whom they loved, and whom we have loved in return. Their serial work, made in the most part for younger audiences, was at its least childish; and at its best, childlike. For kids of the 1920s, the '30s and the '40s, it provided a lot of fun. This book is also dedicated to the young-at-heart movie serial fan of years gone by, and for those today who want to know what all the fuss (not to mention all the fun) was about.

ACKNOWLEDGMENTS

Writing can be the loneliest profession, but most writing worth the reading comes from creative interaction. This book would not be possible without the skills and generosity of a great many people. I have to thank my parents, who let me barge in to work at my Mom's word processor until I could install a rig of my own. I would appear, armed with papers and books, and would work long into the night. They scratched their heads, not understanding, but tolerating the interests of their oldest son. I wish my Dad had lived to see this book. He passed away two days before Halloween 1999. I'd like to think that in Heaven—wherever that is—my Dad might be sitting with actor Clayton Moore and enjoying a chapter from *The Perils of Nyoka*, his favorite serial.

I must thank Gary Don Rhodes for suggesting I do this book in the first place. George Turner and his wife, Jean Wade Turner—both since deceased—offered immeasurable support and encouragement. George's collaborator of more than 30 years, the syndicated film critic, radio personality and film-festival honcho Mike Price, opened up the Turner-Price archives to this book's advantage and contributed helpful streamlining.

Wayne Schutz offered advice and shared hard-to-find information. I recommend his book, *The Motion Picture Serial: An Annotated Bibliography*, to anyone interested in the idiom. Wayne connected me with film-music scholar and conductor Lou McMahon, and with other generous experts, including Jim Stringham, Dr. Bill G. "Buck" Rainey, Ed Billings and Marty Kelly.

Norman Kietzer of *Favorite Westerns & Serials* magazine found copies of many obscure films. Jeff Walton, former publisher of *Serial Report*, supplied helpful information and guidance. Bill Naras helped track down crucial interview subjects.

Ford I. Beebe, Jr., son of the famed serial director and an old Hollywood figure in his own right, supplied comments that have proved crucial. Other helpful background came from the visual-effects pioneer Linwood P. Dunn (1904-1998)—a nephew, by no coincidence, of the pioneering serial director Spencer Gordon Bennet—and from Mr. Bennet's daughter, Harriet Bennet Pessis.

Also helpful were Diana Serra Cary (former child star Baby Peggy Montgomery); actor Russell Wade, who worked with Boris Karloff and Bela Lugosi, and was a friend of Lon Chaney, Jr.; and Mrs. Russell Wade. Additionally, I thank Kate Phillips (aka actress Kay Linaker) and radio historian Frank Brisee.

Madeline Matz at the Library of Congress proved immeasurably helpful in the archival searching. My Washington-area hosts, Jack and Marilyn Smith, helped enable a thorough research trip. Author Brian Taves, encountered at the Library of Congress, took the time to talk about his own findings on Bela Lugosi. Thanks, likewise, to Ron Adams and participants in the 1997 Monster Bash convention, and to Forrest J Ackerman, without whose *Famous Monsters of Filmland* magazine this field of endeavor would be the poorer.

Long-term thanks to Ted Schmitt, formerly of the Universal/16 film-rental office in Chicago, who let me see many wonderful films from his library as I began my own high school years. One of those films was a serial called *The Phantom Creeps*, starring Bela Lugosi. Speaking of *The Phantom Creeps*, I must thank Ronald V. Borst for copying materials from the serial's rare pressbook and its even more scarce comic book version.

Other helping hands: Mike Dobbs of the *Animation Planet* Web site; the "Tuesday Night Group" of the late and truly great Mickey Gold, Charlie and Mildred Hunt, Wally Drewniak and his sister Wanda, and Ralph Garcia and John Bortowski, who all helped me see decent prints of some of the serials; attorney Jim Nally, who offered much-needed advice; my sister-in-law, computer whiz Laurie Axium Kohl; writer and fellow *King Kong* devotee Steve Vertlieb; Chaney scholar Richard Bojarski, who supplied rare stills and information from his collection on Lon Chaney, Jr.'s serials; writer Mark Miller, for helpful suggestions; Republic Pictures expert Jack Mathis; serial historian Jim Shoenberger; director Joseph H. Lewis; Alex Gordon and his brother, Richard; *Filmfax* publisher Mike Stein and former Managing Editor Ted Okuda; Mike Brooks, for emergency computer assistance; Don G. Smith, author of *Lon Chaney, Jr.: Horror Film Star: 1906-1973*; Jon Tuska, author of *The Vanishing Legion: A History of Mascot Pictures; 1927-1935*; the late cartoon animator Gordon Sheehan; Steve Stanchfield—also an animator—who led me to helpful contacts of information including Bill McCrea; Jim Doherty and Keith Folk, who helped track down rare footage on videocassette; writers Greg Mank and Tom Weaver; historian/collector Blackie Seymour; and my fellow office workers: Valleta Smith, Bridget McLaughlin, Cathy Dwyer, Ed George, Mike Buchanan and Andrea Gibson; Eric Stedman of the Serial Squadron Web site; Johanne Tournier of the Lugosiphiles Web site and fellow cohorts like Bill Chase and Fr. Michael Paraniuk; Bob Youhouse and John Johnson.

For tremendous help in finding rare photos and illustrations: Buddy Barnette, Richard Bojarski, Eddie Brandt's Saturday Matinee, Ron Borst, Cinema Collectors, David Graveen, Larry Edmunds' Bookshop, Movie Star News, Jerry Ohlinger's Movie Material Store, *Midnight Marquee* magazine and its parent Midnight Marquee Press, Photofest, Ted Okuda, Gary Don Rhodes, Stephen Sally, Jim Stringham, George Turner and Mike Price.

Finally, for their blessings on this project, my heartfelt thanks to Sara Karloff, Bela G. Lugosi, Jr., and Ron Chaney.

FOREWORD
by George E. Turner

Universal's three most popular stars of horror pictures—Bela Lugosi, Boris Karloff and Lon Chaney, Jr.—also were serial stars. This self-evident truth may come as a surprise to their followers who only remember the actors from their feature films, but it is a fact that each of the fearsome three graced quite a few chapter plays during their long careers. Some writers have mentioned their appearances in the cliffhangers, but these comments have never gone in depth to the extent that Leonard Kohl offers in this pioneering work. His research alone is an enormous undertaking that bespeaks a devotion to the subject and the desire to give freely of what he has learned.

And why, one might wonder, is research on the serials so difficult? Why, simply because critics outside of the show business publications held their noses high and ignored them. The tradepapers sketchily covered trade-show screenings of the first few chapters of some new serials. Popular silent-screen stars such as Pearl White and Ruth Roland were sometimes subjects for the mass-readership press. In the 1930s, though, it was a red-letter day for serial lovers when *Time* and *Look* magazines actually devoted space to *Flash Gordon's Trip to Mars*—and when, on other occasions, *The New York Times* and the *Saturday Evening Post* and *Screen Guide* and *Pic* carried *very occasional* stories about serials. In recent years, decades after the episodic form became extinct, specialized publications about serials have emerged, mostly fan-oriented but usually sincere and thorough.

It was on a windy spring day in 1931 that I saw the posters for Universal's *Dracula* at the Mission Theatre in Amarillo, Texas. They showed a cruel-looking, sharp-featured man in a black cape looming with obvious evil intent over the bed of a blonde beauty. Naturally, I wanted to see the movie, but my mother read to me a "snipe" pasted onto the three-sheet: "This picture will not be of interest to children. NO CHILDREN'S ADMISSIONS SOLD."

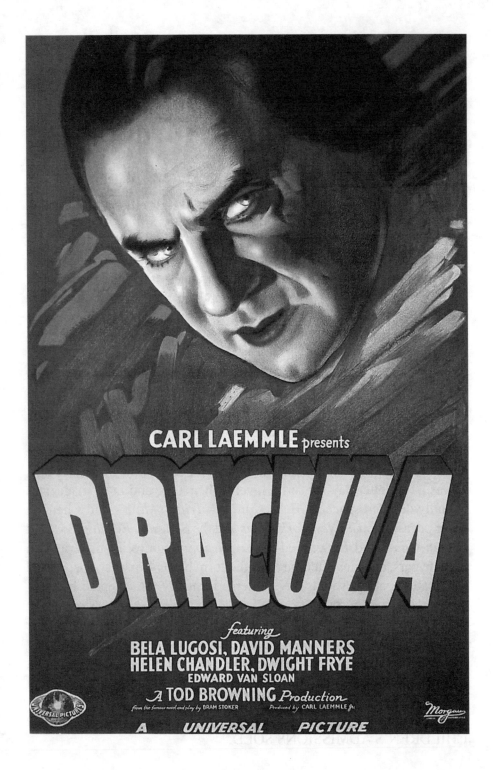

CARL LAEMMLE presents

DRACULA

featuring

BELA LUGOSI, DAVID MANNERS
HELEN CHANDLER, DWIGHT FRYE
EDWARD VAN SLOAN

A TOD BROWNING *Production*

from the famous novel and play by BRAM STOKER   *Produced by* CARL LAEMMLE Jr.

A   UNIVERSAL   PICTURE

"Children" were customers under 12. I was approaching six. Drat!

Thus did I miss out on the performance that made a Hungarian émigré, Bela Lugosi, the first great horror star of the talking pictures. The beloved silent star Lon Chaney, who was especially popular in weird roles, had died recently after making his only talkie. Conrad Veidt, another silent star celebrated for his horror roles in Europe and America, had returned to Europe with a bad case of "mike fright" brought on by his heavy accent. Both men had been considered for *Dracula*, until fate intervened. Lugosi was proclaimed as the successor to these artists. Although he had been an internationally known stage and screen actor, Lugosi the movie star was a creation of talking pictures. His accent was as heavy as Veidt's, but that only added to his sinister charm. *Dracula* was also released to theaters not equipped for sound, and with a sound-on-disc track for theaters still using Vitaphone equipment.

Eight months later, on a freezing December night, my mother took me to the Mission to see a sensational new picture titled *Frankenstein*. On the way, I asked her what it was about. "It's about a giant," she told me, and in my mind's eye I saw a big, hairy brute carrying a club. Moments later we were gazing awe-struck at the gaunt, scarred face and seemingly gigantic black frame of the Monster, whose sunken, heavy-lidded eyes regarded us balefully from the screen. That first close look at the man-made monster was a delightfully harrowing introduction to the man who would become my favorite actor.

After the show, when we were returning to our Model A on a dark, quiet side street, my mother kept looking over her shoulder into the darkness. Finally, she asked me if I heard footsteps behind us. I hadn't, nor could I see anyone following us. She was shivering before we reached the car. It wasn't the Monster's fearsome appearance that had rattled her; it was the sound of his clumping feet just before the celebrated close-up! The talkies hadn't been around very long at that time, and we hadn't previously encountered a movie in which the sound of ominous footsteps was exploited for menace. It's been done so often since then that nobody even notices.

So it was that a second great horror star was born into the age of the talking cinema. Actually, Karloff had been a rather obscure film actor for about a dozen years. I had seen Karloff a couple of times before, but didn't suspect it was the same man. Once was in another trailblazing "talkie," *King of the Kongo* (1929), which happened to be the first talk-

ing serial. Actually, it was what they called a sound-with-dialogue or "part-talking" picture. That is, it had music (including a theme song), radio-style sound effects and occasional snippets of dialogue, all recorded on discs. Karloff was the chief red herring, an evil-looking guy who everybody assumes is the secret villain, but who turns out to be the girl's long-lost father while an innocuous-looking character is the real fiend. I'd also seen him as a sympathetic outlaw in an all-talking Rex Lease Western, *The Utah Kid* (1930) and—only a couple of months before *Frankenstein*—as a villainous Arab in the all-talking serial, *King of the Wild*. This was the last of several serials in which Karloff performed before *Frankenstein* made him unaffordable for serial budgets.

I caught up with Lugosi the following year, relishing his wonderful, over-the-top performances in *White Zombie* and *Chandu the Magician*.

And in 1938, I finally saw *Dracula*. It was one of those legend-making, green-tinted prints that some know-it-alls insist never existed. And phooey to them from me!

The third popular Universal horror star of the talkies was Creighton Chaney, son of the great Lon, who signed a contract with RKO Radio in 1932. Creighton had supporting roles in several RKO features and was starred in the studio's only serial release, *The Last Frontier* (1932). His option was dropped because he refused to let RKO bill him as Lon Chaney, Jr. As a free-lance, he went on to supporting roles in several serials, and also did some stunt work and played Western heavies, bits, dance extras and whatever else he could find. Two sparsely shown starring pictures for a Poverty Row studio went unnoticed. One, *Scream in the Night* (1936), proved a harbinger of things to come. In this one, the rechristened Lon, Jr. did a good job of playing two characters, one of whom wore a grotesque make-up designed by Junior himself.

When Chaney finally made the big-time at the turn of the decade following his sensational stage and screen performances in *Of Mice and Men*, he landed important roles in *One Million B.C.*, *Man Made Monster* and especially *The Wolf Man*. He probably assumed he was through with serials and Western heavies, but there were more of both in his future even while Universal was proclaiming him to be "the Screen's Master Character Creator."

Most actors tried to avoid being cast in serials because serials were the step-children of the studios. The budgets and schedules were never sufficient for the amount of film that had to be put in the can, which meant long, frantic hours of toil. Why the serial makers were treated so badly is a mystery, because serials were the one class of production that could invariably be depended upon to bring in a healthy profit.

Karloff did all his serial work before he became a star. All of Lugosi's serial roles followed his star turn in *Dracula*. Chaney started as a serial star, fell to ever-smaller supporting roles, eventually made his mark by carrying some memorable features, and then returned to more cliffhanging. How this all came to be is reported admirably by Mr. Kohl. As a lifelong fan of both the serials and the three terrors, I feel honored at the opportunity to bid this landmark work welcome.

George E. Turner
Hollywood, 1998

Sinister Serials

PREFACE

From one actor's point of view, the serials were enjoyable—"but I couldn't help but wonder if they were a sort of dead end," as Clayton Moore told it in his Lone Ranger-and-beyond autobiography, *I Was That Masked Man*. "Few real movie stars started out in serials—John Wayne is a notable exception," Moore added. "It was almost as though, once the industry pegged you as a serial actor, they couldn't see you in any other light."

From the vantage of an agent to the stars and stars-in-waiting, "Serials were a dirty word," as Al Kingston told one of John Wayne's many biographers, Maurice Zolotow.

From a movie director's perspective, starting out with the two- and three-reel comedy shorts in old Hollywood was "pretty much the bottom of the ladder," as veteran *Three Stooges* series helmer Ed Bernds told me in 1996, adding: "At Columbia studios there was only one rung lower than that—that was the serials."

And from the son of a great serial director, Ford I. Beebe, Jr.:

> Directors were cast in much the same manner as actors... If a studio had a suspense script, they hoped to get Hitchcock. If it were an epic, they might try for DeMille. But if it happened to be a serial, they would probably pass up both of the above to get my Dad.

The elder Ford Beebe also handled the entertaining *Bomba the Jungle Boy* pictures for producer Walter Mirisch and directed and/or produced some notable features for Universal, including *Son of Dracula* in 1943. But it is as a director of Westerns and serials that Beebe remains best known—notably, his co-director hitches on some of the classic *Flash Gordon* chapter plays.

From the outlook of film scholarship, we learn from Jim Harmon and Donald F. Glut that:

The A pictures had more spectacle, yes. Serials could not afford massive armies pitted against each other. But the spectacles of major films borrowed on the skills of serial-makers. The classic example may be the fact that the burning of Atlanta and other spectacles in *Gone With the Wind*

were actually directed by second-unit chief
B. Reeves Eason, who directed Tom Mix's
only talking serial, *The Miracle Rider.*

And from the standpoint of an early-day radio announcer: "I grew up surrounded by a variety of heroes, all displaying great courage in the face of untold dangers. Some came to life every Saturday afternoon at the movies in those cliff-hanging serials that always had you coming back for more," as Fred Foy wrote in notes accompanying a Smithsonian Institution collection of radio Western programs. Foy is better known for his timeless narration of the classic radio show, as he invited listeners to "Return with us now to those thrilling days of yesteryear. The Lone Ranger Rides Again!"

For anyone who believes that the movie serials are antiques, with no bearing on what's going on, I must point not only to the modern-day adventure films—which still use much of the narrative grammar of the old-time chapter plays—but also to many of the shows produced for television. The serials live on in different forms, including children's shows like *Mighty Morphin Power Rangers*, daytime soap operas and miniseries epics like *Lonesome Dove*, right on up to such prime-time regulars as *ER*, *NYPD Blue* and *Law and Order*. All these owe much of their suspenseful excitement and virtually all of their episodic plot structures to the movie serials of half a century and more ago.

Ford Beebe, Jr., son of one of the greatest serial directors of the sound era, tried to put the movie serial into its proper perspective in film history in a series of conversations:

> Well, when you peel the finish off the stuff, actually it's more the social interests which are the things that have changed the appearance of the thing [the movie serial], a lot more than the subject matter or the basic premise, you know? At least, that's my feeling, that people today aren't quite as interested in the directness and 'let the good guys win' as they were at the time those [serials] were made. All those subjects that are criticized on TV for having

too much violence, are very similar in a way [to the serials], except that instead of [characters] carrying a sidearm like they did in the '30s, they now carry big automatic flame-throwers or something like that! They're still working on the same ideas!

The serials, in a way, were very like some of the series that are on TV today. The character actors that played the leading parts got to know the characters so well, they didn't have to be directed. They knew what the character was doing, see? And how he would go at whatever he was going at. Of course they got that way through the help of directors, not always the same ones, of course. My recollection of my Dad... he tried the best he could with whatever was presented to him, and that didn't apply only to [directing or writing] pictures. If he had something to do, he would do it the best he could with the circumstances that were provided. And he went at motion pictures that way. One of my Dad's favorite axioms was, "If a thing is worth doing, it's worth doing as well as you can." And he applied this to his work.

For younger readers who might vaguely recognize the names of those horror-movie icons, Boris Karloff, Bela Lugosi and Lon Chaney, Jr., but don't know what a serial is, I'll explain it in brief: Walk into just about any large video store, and you might notice a shelf of larger-than-usual cassette sleeves, labeled "Serials." Each serial is a collection of chapters or episodes, adding up to a single adventurous yarn. In the course of 10 to 15 chapters, ranging from about 12 to 30 minutes apiece, a story is told. These silent serials were popular from around the time of World War I into the late 1920s. Then, the serials were retooled more as entertainment for children, and they remained in production until the middle

"PANIC IN THE ZOO"

Chapter 12

THE GREEN HORNET

with

GORDON JONES as Britt Reid

WADE BOTELER as Michael Axford

KEYE LUKE as Kato

ANNE NAGEL as Miss Case

1950s, when rising production costs and the advent of television—making its own type of serial—finally killed off this part of the film industry.

My Mom grew up in a small town called Waterbury in Connecticut. Her Dad, my Grandfather, lost much of his savings during the Depression, and even worse, my Grandmother died when my mother was still practically a baby. My Grandfather had to raise four girls as best as he could. What that meant, of course, was that going to the movies was a special event. So getting the chance to see *Snow White and the Seven Dwarfs* (1937) or *The Wizard of Oz* (1939) was a very big deal to my Mom.

My Dad was born in Chicago, and even though just about everyone in his neighborhood faced hard times, he always managed to scrape up a dime for the Saturday Matinee. (When admission went up to 11 or 12 cents around the time America entered World War II, that really played heck with the kids' finances!) For a quarter, you could buy candy, a soda pop and a ticket for an all-day show. My Dad loved the rough-and-tumble cowboy pictures. He grew up as an admirer of John Wayne, Gary Cooper, Hopalong Cassidy and Tom Mix (his early sound Westerns were still being shown)—but steered clear of the singing-cowboy pictures. Westerns were so popular with kids that in the 1930s and '40s some theaters like the Roscoe—on the northwest side of Chicago—showed nothing *but* Westerns for years. Depending on the theater, you could be treated to a *Sherlock Holmes* film, or a *Tarzan* film, or an *East Side Kids* comedy. In the neighborhood theaters, short subjects were part of the standard package, and generally this included serials.

Movie serials were shown once a week, although many neighborhood movie houses made a practice of running the first chapter of a new serial following the concluding chapter of the serial that had been running for the past few months. This practice was a great way for kids to stay hooked on coming to the theater week after week. Brothers Mickey and Eddie Gold once told me that during a flu epidemic in Chicago 1940, many theaters were closed for weeks. When the theaters finally re-opened, the boys were in Serial Heaven as one movie house showed not one but *four* chapters of *Flash Gordon Conquers the Universe*, just to make up for lost time.

One of my Dad's favorite serials was *The Perils of Nyoka* (1942), an above-average Republic production. Although it had Clayton Moore as the hero, Kay Aldridge as the beautiful heroine, Lorna Gray as a voluptuous villain and the great Charles Middleton as her nasty sidekick, the real star of the show to my Dad and his friends was the villain's pet

Chapter **1**
DESERT INTRIGUE

PERILS OF NYOKA
A REPUBLIC SERIAL in 15 chapters

KAY ALDRIDGE
The Serial Queen
CLAYTON MOORE
WILLIAM BENEDICT
LORNA GRAY
CHARLES MIDDLETON
WILLIAM WITNEY-DIRECTOR
ORIGINAL SCREEN PLAY BY RONALD DAVIDSON
NORMAN S. HALL • WILLIAM LIVELY
JOSEPH O'DONNELL • JOSEPH POLAND

gorilla, Satan. Those kids rooted for the not-entirely-realistic creature for week after week. It bears mentioning here that Steven Spielberg and

12 New DYNAMIC CHAPTERS

THE New UNIVERSAL
presents

FLASH GORDON
CONQUERS THE UNIVERSE

with

LARRY "Buster" CRABBE as FLASH GORDON
CAROL HUGHES as DALE ARDEN
ANNE GWYNNE as SONJA
CHARLES MIDDLETON as EMPEROR MING
FRANK SHANNON as DR. ZARKOV

George Lucas' 1981 hit, *Raiders of the Lost Ark*, took considerable inspiration from *The Perils of Nyoka*.

By the early 1950s, when most of the serials began airing on television—especially the *Flash Gordon* adventures—youngsters including

George Lucas and Steven Spielberg saw them run generally once a week, on Saturdays, just as their parents might have seen them. Most people in my neighborhood did not have color television sets until the late 1960s. Many of the TV programs and movies shown on TV were filmed in black-and-white anyway, so it didn't matter much if the movie we saw was a couple of years old or 30 years old. Youngsters in the early TV era, even through most of the 1970s, enjoyed the same comedies, Westerns, cartoons and serials that their parents had enjoyed on the big screen. Today, with cable TV and home-video technology taken for granted, the serials pop up regularly—but their black-and-white clarity and straightforward melodrama, in a culture attuned to livid color and nonlinear flashcut editing, causes a distancing effect that has obliterated the urgency and immediacy that the first-generation television audiences derived from the older films.

When the studios began marketing videocassettes of movies, it was only natural that some of the better serials should become available. Because many studios sold the rights to television or theatrical distribution companies, and often forgot to renew their copyrights, many serials fell into the public domain. This means that any company can distribute copies of these serials, even if the film's original studio possesses the master footage but declines to use or license it. Thus, many smaller dealers will peddle inferior copies—often making it difficult to judge a serial fairly. Anchor Bay Entertainment worked hard to get permission from the owners of the *Green Hornet* characters, and also called upon the source-studio, Universal Pictures, to find well-preserved 35-millimeter elements of the 1940 serial, *The Green Hornet Strikes Again*. The sound-and-picture quality on Anchor Bay's video edition is generally outstanding, showing considerable care in presentation. On the other hand, I have never seen anything *close* to a decent copy of Universal's *The Phantom Creeps*, which dates from only a year earlier, 1939.

Fortunately, there are beautiful prints of many other serials on videocassette. Never mind that a movie serial really belongs on a big screen, shown in chapters once a week to a crowd of youngsters and overgrown youngsters-at-heart, . The movie serial, more than any other type of film, truly reflects the values and prejudices of its era. The idiom is living history in the truest sense, and in order to understand the culture today, we must know what our prior generations enjoyed.

Those of you who have never seen a serial, and who want to know what they are all about, should not get your hopes up too high. You may find them silly, old-fashioned, politically incorrect, and perhaps even boring. They were made for kids—generally speaking, boys—in the first half of the 20th century. It helps to watch a chapter or two at a time, never an entire serial in one sitting.

Those who grew up watching, say, *Land of the Lost* in the late 1970s, or more recent fare like *Mighty Morphin Power Rangers*, might enjoy the serials. Ditto for *Star Trek*, and the *Die Hard* or *Under Siege* feature-film series, and—of course—the *Star Wars* and *Indiana Jones* adventures. Of all the movies that came out as I was compiling this collection, *The Mask of Zorro* (1998) proved the strongest evocation of some of the best serials Republic Pictures ever made, among them *Zorro Rides Again* (1937), *Zorro's Fighting Legion* (1939) and *The Ghost of Zorro* (1949).

Just as viewers of Nick at Nite or TV Land enjoy spotting modern-day stars in small roles on early-day television shows, you'll find famous actors like John Wayne or Clayton "Lone Ranger" Moore on their way up in the serials. You'll also spot actors like Lee J. Cobb and Leonard Nimoy in small roles. Serials were a proving ground for up-and-coming actors, and often a refuge for fading stars. Any number of television shows have held fast to this principle: The *Perry Mason* series, with Raymond Burr, always seemed to have a lot of familiar faces from bygone days, and newcomers destined for bigger things, as well.

Star-watching is really the whole intent of this book. If you are a fan of Boris Karloff's work, the opportunity to backtrack to his performances before *Frankenstein* will be extremely interesting. Seeing Bela Lugosi in the serials, during the period where his prestige started to drop and then began to rise anew, will no doubt appeal to Lugosi's fans. The struggle for acceptance that lay ahead for Creighton Chaney is all there for the watching in his serial work dating from 1932, which should be fascinating for devotees of the actor whom Hollywood rechristened Lon Chaney, Jr.

At the start of the 20th century, Americans were growing accustomed not only to the horseless carriage, but also to the telephone, the phonograph and the movies. The world had grown smaller as a consequence of intensified communications, from daily newspapers to the telegraph, telephone and radio, not to mention a vastly improved mail service. Parents worried about the effects that the dime novel and its upstart spin-off, the

pulp magazine, the newspapers' comic strips, and the sometimes shocking motion pictures might be having on their children. As the century

wore on, newer technologies from television to tape recorders brought additional concerns about positive or negative effects. People suddenly had access to more and more forms of entertainment, whether for good or for ill.

What might be shocking to some parents might be perfectly all right for others. So although my Dad didn't grow up watching *Dracula*, *Frankenstein* or *King Kong* or reading superheroic comic books, he was permitted to see adventure films, cartoons and particularly Westerns. No doubt, his strong sense of right and wrong was strengthened by watching countless cowboy movies, where the hero saved the day and the villain got what was coming to him. I like to believe that I have some of the same values, even though television, a kind of time machine, enabled me to see the kinds of films—particularly the horror movies—that Dad hadn't been permitted to see.

What did I learn from watching these Depression-era monster movies, a generation after their debuts? Well, I certainly felt compassion for Karloff's Frankenstein Monster, and for Junior Chaney's tormented werewolf, Larry Talbot. The perceptibly bad things that the Monster does are done out of fear and anger, not out of any calculated evil scheme. He is lonely, frightened and misunderstood. The Wolf Man lapses out of control when the moon turns full. As my friend Mike Brooks has put it, the Wolf Man is probably the most frightening of monsters, for he was once one of us. Lugosi's Count Dracula and Karloff's Mummy are creatures of thoroughgoing evil, but even they have admirable qualities, not the least of which is a shared streak of romanticism.

The best of the monster movies are morality plays, a constant struggle between good and evil. These earlier films may not be as frightening as the newer scare shows, but they retain a power that is beyond the grasp of the shock value usurpers. Did seeing these films change our lives for the better? I'd like to think that they did.

Ray Bradbury's parents thought that there were worse things that their son could enjoy than frightening films such as 1925's *The Phantom of the Opera* and comic strips like *Buck Rogers*. These had a tremendous impact on young Bradbury, who grew up to become one of our most humane and spellbinding writers of science fiction and fantasy. Bradbury's friend, Ray Harryhausen, was captivated by the animated stop-motion monsters of *The Lost World* (1925) and, especially, *King Kong* (1933), and began his career in earnest by working alongside his idol, master animator Willis O'Brien, on another ape-escape gem, *Mighty Joe Young* (1949). A youngster by the name of George Turner was also captivated by *King Kong*, which had a profound effect on his career. Many years later, George wrote *The Making of King Kong* in collaboration with Orville Goldner, one of *Kong*'s technicians. Buster Crabbe once noted with pride that the Apollo 11 astronauts had acknowledged Crabbe's star turns in the *Flash Gordon* serials as an inspiration.

I can trace the beginnings of my fascination to a snowy evening late in December 1966. I was visiting my grandparents at their apartment, where I sat with my brother Jerry and our cousin Joey, watching a cartoon based on Dr. Seuss' *How the Grinch Stole Christmas!* The voice of the Grinch, and the narrator of the story, was someone by the name of Boris Karloff, who I had been told had played monsters in the movies. Some years later, when I was in fourth grade, I believe, our teacher let us watch CBS' *Morning News*. On the broadcast, I saw a film clip of a scary-looking monster, screaming in terror and pain, trapped in a burning windmill. The newscaster said that the actor Boris Karloff had just died. Who the heck *was* that? I had to know! Not too long after that, WGN-TV in Chicago ran a series of old horror films under the blanket title *Creature Features*. That fascination has never really left me.

As I grew older, I realized that Karloff, Lugosi and Chaney were not just images on a movie or television screen. Lugosi's tragic but sometimes joyous life intrigued me. The more I read about Karloff and certainly, about Chaney, the more I realized that there were terrible times in their lives as well. The popularly beloved Karloff had struggled against obscurity. The downtrodden Lugosi occasionally had a run of good luck and was sometimes allowed to show that he really could be one fine actor. Junior Chaney was a sad, frustrated man, but he also had his brighter moments and got along well with the people who accepted him on his own terms. I learned to appreciate the actors for who they were, not just for the illusions they created.

We had no idea of the age of some of the shows we used to watch, for the black-and-white TV screen is a powerful equalizer and few broadcasting stations have bothered with such niceties as historical context. The worn-out, re-titled, old-looking films exercised a fascination for me, and I imagine, for many other kids like me, the offspring and grandchildren of the Depression-era kids for whom many of the serials were originally intended. I became keen on learning how the serials were made, and I grew to appreciate the fact that, all these years later, they still influenced shows like *Lost in Space* and *Star Trek*. When I was away at college, I found out that one of my childhood television heroes, Buster Crabbe, Flash Gordon himself, would be appearing at a special show back home in Chicago. A bad cold, a few hundred miles and some overdue term papers were not going to keep me from meeting him—but that's another story.

Three actors, who played some of the most memorable monsters and villains in movie history, all made serials. For Boris Karloff, his work in the serials took place when he was a struggling actor. His last serial, *King of the Wild*, was made early in 1931. No one knew, least of all Karloff himself, that he would become a star less than a year later, via *Frankenstein*. For Bela Lugosi, the serials were made from the time his prominence had begun to erode and, all too briefly, to rise again. Lugosi's last serial, *The Phantom Creeps*, was made shortly after his triumphant comeback as Ygor in *Son of Frankenstein*. For Lon Chaney, Jr., the serial work started soon after he had dedicated himself to an acting career. Like Karloff and Lugosi, Chaney knew some very tough years in Hollywood. Chaney's last two serials were made just as he was gaining acceptance as the new horror-film star at Universal. His short-lived stardom was mainly due to his role of a sympathetic man turned into an electrified zombie in *Man Made Monster* (1941), and by his unforgettable performance in *The Wolf Man* (1941).

This period in Hollywood moviemaking, from 1918 to 1942, is a pivotal stretch of history. It covers a time when America asserted itself as a social and cultural force to be reckoned with, a period between the end of World War I and the early years of America's involvement in World War II. It was a time of prosperity and then of a terrible Depression that lasted over 10 years. For the Hollywood studios, it was when filmmaking had emerged as an art form, to a period of confusion over the upheaval provoked by talking pictures, and finally to what film buffs tend to characterize as a Golden Age of cinema. For English actor Boris Karloff, the era was one of an upward struggle toward stardom. For Hungarian actor Bela Lugosi, the period was one of fantastic change: A star in his own country escapes to America during a Communist uprising, and struggles to become a star on Broadway and in the movies, with more ups and downs than a roller coaster. For Lon Chaney, Jr., the son of a brilliant silent-screen actor, it was a time of painstaking, and never thoroughly successful, efforts to dodge the shadow of his father while honoring his father's memory. This, then, is a long-obscured region that wants exploring. I have sought to convey a sense of not only how, but also *why* these serials were made.

For serials that are readily accessible to the home-video enthusiast, I have given the briefest of synopses. For serials considered lost, I've indulged in more thorough versions of the story, often from scant materials. I have also gone into more detail with *The Hope Diamond Mystery* (1921), which *does* exist, but only in institutional archival form.

Leonard J. Kohl
January 2000

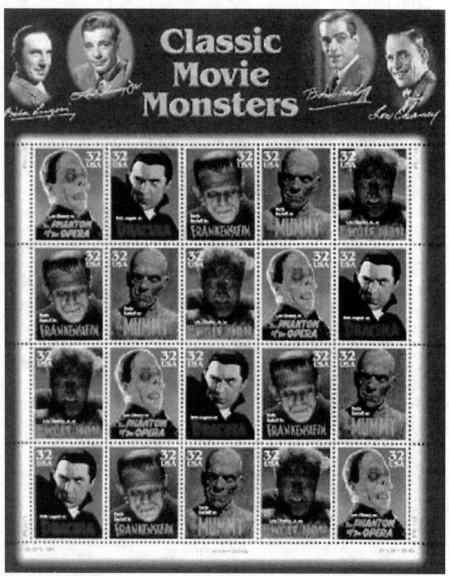

In 1997 the U.S. Postal Service honored Lon Chaney, Jr. and Sr., Boris Karloff and Bela Lugosi with stamps depicting their most famous movie characters.

CHAPTER ONE
Frankenstein's Monster, Count Dracula and the Wolf Man: From Picture Screens To Postage Stamps

Motion pictures are filmed "in a disconnected way and then spliced together," as Maurice Zolotow nailed the process in his biography of John Wayne, *Shooting Star*. Zolotow explained that "movie acting depends on mastery of one's body and emotions and imagination to such a degree that one can instantaneously turn oneself on like a light switch."

The observation bears considering in view of the performances of Boris Karloff, Bela Lugosi and Lon Chaney, Jr. in their serials: A production schedule often called for 50 to 100 camera set-ups a day.

Of course, it also helps to remember that John Wayne was primarily a film actor—one who found his few turns on stage "a pain, y'know, the pure unrelieved stress of 'being somebody else' without so much as a breather between speeches," as Wayne told George Turner and Michael H. Price in 1968.

Boris Karloff, conversely, was a stage actor turned screen actor. Karloff had acted in films for over 10 years before he garnered massed critical notice and popular recognition as a standout in Howard Hawks' *The Criminal Code* and James Whale's *Frankenstein*, both in 1931. In an interview during the middle 1930s, Karloff told of how he had learned to scale down his work to deal with the camera:

> I am always myself until the moment I face
> the camera. I do not believe it is necessary
> for an actor to pace up and down the set,
> sometimes hours before he is ready to take

Boris Karloff, c. 1931

a scene, screwing up his face, gesticulating and physically rehearsing over and over again. Personally, I have found the best results by memorizing my lines and actions mentally and producing the physical reaction when I am at work.

It isn't that I have any particular aversion to rehearsing; on the contrary, I study and memorize every line that I have to speak and every gesture I have to create, but I do it with a minimum of physical effort. I find myself better able to grasp a situation and character by the sole method of concentration.

It is interesting that Karloff could master the art of acting before a movie camera, but took a long time to get over a case of stage fright when he appeared on Broadway in *Arsenic and Old Lace* in 1941. His cordial rival, Bela Lugosi, had triumphed on Broadway in 1927, and often granted that he felt more at home on the boards than on a movie set. For Lugosi was even more genuinely a stage actor, an actor accustomed to overplaying a performance so that the entire audience could enjoy its full measure. But by the time he appeared in *Dracula* (1931), Lugosi had logged considerable screen time, too. Stage actors get into character shortly before a play begins, and they stay in that psychological state—many players call it the Zone—until they take their curtain calls. Screen actor Clayton Moore's reminiscences of Lugosi are revealing, and typical of remarks from many others who worked with Lugosi. Moore wrote in his autobiography, *I Was That Masked Man*:

> Of course, he was nothing like the roles he played. Instead, Lugosi was very polite and reserved... He wasn't unfriendly; he just wasn't very talkative. Lugosi was also well rehearsed and meticulous... didn't react well if you just asked him to change something on the spur of the moment. Lugosi was a fine actor, I know that, and nice to work with.

The stage training had conditioned Lugosi to keep to himself while on the set in order to stay in character. Karloff had learned the art of switching on and off. Under a capable director, and given the time to analyze his character—as Lugosi managed to do with the role of Ygor in *Son of Frankenstein* (1939)—the actor could tone down his performance for the camera. But he never strayed far from the stagebound professional background.

This contrast holds true, as well, with one of the great comedy teams, Laurel and Hardy. Stan Laurel learned his craft on the music-hall stages of England, honed it in American Vaudeville, and then, years later, began acting in films. As a comedian, but also as a stage actor, Laurel learned how to play to an audience. He learned to exaggerate his presence, so that anyone seated anywhere in the auditorium would get the drift. Where Oliver Hardy had been a singer and actor in the Southern U.S. minstrel tradition and, later, in Vaudeville, he learned most of his acting skills in the presence of the camera. Hardy learned how to give his presence a greater subtlety, having learned how the camera magnified him.

This is hardly to say that Laurel did not understand the chemistry of movies, for the teaming of his broader style with Hardy's genteel manner was a deliberate and masterful strategy, of which both comedians were more or less equally in control. In a late-in-life interview in 1992, their chief producer, Hal Roach, told Michael H. Price that it was Laurel who harbored the greater ambitions to become a producer in his own right, and who contributed the greater measure of visual gags to the act. Hardy, Roach said, nurtured the team's crucial play-on-words routines and encouraged the greater use of the Laurel and Hardy pictures' crowd-pleasing musical interludes. If we might characterize the occasional teamings of Karloff and Lugosi as the horror movies' equivalent of Laurel and Hardy, then Stan Laurel would have more in common with Lugosi where Karloff might show a similarity to Oliver Hardy, each in terms of acting technique. For each team boasts a pleasing mixture of opposites-in-attraction styles.

Lon Chaney, Jr. poses a greater paradox. While both Karloff and Lugosi had known tough times in their early years, Junior's beginnings were probably tougher, at least in the psychological sense. Neither Karloff nor Lugosi had a world-famous Hollywood star for a father. And throughout his working career, the younger Chaney would constantly be measured against the legacy of his sire.

"Do me a favor, will you?" Creighton Chaney—who had yet to accept the "Lon, Jr." identity—asked of film journalist Nancy Pryor during an interview for the January 1933 issue of *Movie Classic* magazine. "If you are going to write me up in a story, don't say anything comparing me with my father. There isn't any comparison between us. Dad was an artist—a real actor. I'm just a fellow trying to get along in the movies.

Lon Chaney, Jr.

I'd rather be compared to anybody else but my dad, because I know I'm not worthy of the comparison."

Chaney continued: "I would never be big enough, or enough of an artist to make the sacrifices my dad did. In the first place, I haven't his great talent for make-up and characterization—so I couldn't if I wanted to."

The Pryor article tells us that Junior knew full well what might lie in store for him, even so early in his career. Lon Chaney had been a titan of

Bela Lugosi, c. 1931

screen drama who cast his shadow before him, never behind. It was a sweeping, even intimidating, shadow that projected from beyond the grave, and the son could never escape its swath. As for making sacrifices for the sake of a career, the son patently followed in his father's path and never mind the hardships. In terms of acting ability, perhaps the younger

Chaney would not measure up to his father's standards of versatility and immersion in craft, but Junior earned what success he did meet, whether as a star in his own right or as a dependable character player. Karloff and Lugosi both left home at early ages as self-exiles, worked at hard labor when there were no acting opportunities, and became theatrical and cinematic professionals against the wishes of their families. But neither did they suffer the disadvantage of having a famous family member looming over their chosen field of endeavor.

Creighton Chaney had covered the works, from stunt action to bit parts in films, for years. But it was the grueling demands of stage work (particularly in the West Coast stage production of John Steinbeck's *Of Mice and Men*) that whipped him into shape as an actor. Also, like Karloff, Chaney learned how to turn on and off during an assignment, but he could match Lugosi at the task of getting into character. The one thing Lon Chaney, Jr. lacked was the unquestioned dramatic authority to carry a film by himself. And yet most people who have seen *Of Mice and Men* and *The Wolf Man* will remember Junior more vividly than any other of those ensembles' players.

It bears remembering that we Americans tend to like our villains and monsters-in-spite-of-themselves to be somewhat foreign, people different from us in some way—from Karloff and Lugosi and Peter Lorre, in old Hollywood, right on up to such choice miscreants of recent times as *Die Hard*'s Alan Rickman and *Con Air*'s Danny Trejo. Perhaps Chaney, Jr. was too all-American in aspect, too much like us, to become a commandingly exotic presence on the screen. And yet, that very robust all-Americanism makes his portrayal of Larry Talbot unforgettable in *The Wolf Man* and its sequels.

The main reason a Lugosi fan enjoys a cheap film like *The Devil Bat* (1940) or *The Corpse Vanishes* (1942) is because of that carefully sustained starring persona, which renders immaterial a film's studio pedigree. I would rather view a spirited Lugosi cavorting in one of his low-rent items, than watch a lackluster film like *Voodoo Island* (1957), with an indifferent performance from Karloff. There are Karloff fans, of course, who would rather watch a leaden leading performance in *The Climax* (1944) or the *Mr. Wong* series, than sit through *The Ape Man*, with Lugosi. There are Chaney fans who would watch Junior gnaw the scenery in *The Alligator People* (1959) rather than see a patently bored Karloff in *Frankenstein 1970* (1958) or a lethargic Lugosi in *Genius at Work* (1946).

I could go on and on with this game, but for the distraction of an interesting thought: Would Karloff or Lugosi, in a more youthful near-prime, have been as good in the leading role of *Strange Confession* (1945) as the still-youthful Chaney is in that very film? Certainly, when portraying a scientist driven mad by indignities, Karloff or Lugosi could handle the character with ease. But how about the happy-go-lucky family man whom Junior portrays with such natural ease in the early reels of *Strange Confession*?

On the other hand, I am of the opinion that Chaney was a wrong choice, much as Karloff would have been a wrong choice, to play the lead in *Son of Dracula* (1943). And why so? Precisely because the persona of Dracula—from the 1927 Broadway play to the 1931 movie version and beyond—rests on the very personality of Bela Lugosi. Chaney has his moments in *Son of Dracula*, but he lacks the mystique, foreign or otherwise, that the role requires.

Popular perception is a strange force, as shallow as it is narrow and yet overwhelmingly powerful: It will define an actor like Lugosi as weird in the public view, when in fact surviving interview footage and still-emerging details of the actor's life off-screen prove Lugosi to have been a hard-working, good-humored and dedicated professional who fully understood the advantages and drawbacks of his lifelong typecasting.

Boris Karloff, in a 1968 interview with George Turner and Mike Price, lamented similar misperceptions about his own life-vs.-career image:

> The perception is the dark opposite of the reality. Ever since that fateful bit of casting in 1931—and you *know* the one I mean—the people *en masse* have actually been predisposed to believe that I must be some manner of monster. As many kindly deeds as I have performed for charity, as many phonograph records for children as I have narrated, as often as I have been seen in public in the benevolent company of Shirley Temple and Danny Kaye and Red Skelton, for goodness' sake, people still see me and think, "Frankenstein!"

Karloff was grateful for the shadow of the Frankenstein Monster, for it had helped make him a star. But this role did not smother Karloff in the way Count Dracula had absorbed Bela Lugosi, or in the way that Lon Chaney, the elder, had inadvertently left Junior saddled with self-doubts. Karloff understood the Monster, whose nature as an outsider mirrored the alienation Karloff had felt as a youngster bent upon becoming an actor against the wishes of his family. In 1933, during a trip to England to film *The Ghoul*, Karloff was surprised and delighted when, in a reunion with his brothers and other kin, he learned that they were proud of his success.

More so than the Frankenstein Monster suited Karloff or the Wolf Man matched Chaney, the image of *Dracula*'s demon lover fit Lugosi like a second skin. Not only Lugosi's sonorous Hungarian accent, but also his commanding personality became essential to the popular image of Count Dracula. While Lugosi tried to get other roles, the moviemakers and their audiences saw Bela Lugosi only in that identity. As late as the 1940s, the low-rent producer Sam Katzman was touting Lugosi as "Mr. Dracula," and never mind that Lugosi played nary a vampire during his lengthy association with Katzman. There were certainly times when Karloff, like Lugosi, fiercely resented his typecasting. Certainly, Chaney resented many of the monstrous parts and takeoffs on *Of Mice and Men* that he would find himself obliged to play. However, there were times when both Karloff and Chaney found a chance to play characters apart from the popular expectations. It becomes a joy to see a television piece like "The Golden Junkman" (1956)—from the weekly anthology, *Telephone Time*—in which Chaney plays an unlettered immigrant who wants only the best for his sons. It is a joy to watch Karloff tear into a role like the drolly sociopathic John Gray in *The Body Snatcher* (1945) or hear him give voice to the title miscreant in *How the Grinch Stole Christmas!* (1966). Lugosi could have played a role of the "Golden Junkman" variety, and his cynical, defiant Ygor of *Son of Frankenstein* and *The Ghost of Frankenstein* would have much in common with John Gray. Of course, after the 1930s, Lugosi very seldom got the chance to prove his greater worth as an actor.

We can put some of the blame on Lugosi himself. If Lugosi had worked harder at mastering the English language, and had he been a bit more cautious about filtering the roles offered to him, particularly in the early 1930s, we might have more classic performances of his to enjoy.

Some of this blame can be directed at the agents in Lugosi's employ; they hardly marketed their client as well as he deserved. Had Lugosi's agent held out for more money for *Dracula*, or seen the wisdom of longer-term contracts measured in years rather than in number of films, things might have worked out better.

Karloff himself had frustrating times in Hollywood. Like most of his fellow actors, he worked incredibly long hours in films before the formation of the Screen Actors Guild, which he and Lugosi helped to establish. Karloff often found himself in films that wasted his talents—but in all, things worked out rather well for him. Certainly in later interviews, Karloff often exulted in his good fortune over the long haul.

Junior Chaney felt driven to honor if not match the fame of a late-and-lamented father. *The Wolf Man*'s tragic would-be hero, Larry Talbot, is a role that captures something of Junior's very being. Talbot is an outsider, trying to come home and striving to prove his worth to his father (Claude Rains). Like John Wayne's character of Sean Thornton in *The Quiet Man* (1952), outsider Larry Talbot seeks out his homeland and wins the affections of a village beauty, but Sean Thornton loses neither love nor life. It is tempting to read too much into Chaney's performances, but still his troubled roles in both *The Wolf Man* and *Of Mice and Men* are clearly Chaney's most personally felt roles.

Like Lugosi, Chaney was dogged by a drinking problem, which limited the kinds of roles he would be given as the years went by. There are conflicting accounts as to how well Chaney and Lugosi got along. If there was rancor, it is a sad thing, because their lives became very similar. Karloff thought the world of Junior's father, but he and the younger Chaney never really became close friends. When they met for *House of Frankenstein* in the middle '40s, Karloff cannot have been unaware of how shoddily Universal Pictures had treated its lucrative monster characters in the days since Karloff had held sway at the big studio during the '30s. The two stars kept a cordial relationship, but not a tremendously friendly one. Chaney—like Lugosi—could be boisterous and fun-loving, but only as a rule with people whom he knew well. Perhaps Chaney was too different in temperament from Karloff. Chaney, like Karloff, could walk through an assignment he didn't much care for. And yet when excited about a role, he would work at it with all the enthusiasm that Karloff or especially Lugosi would likewise give. Karloff seemed to respect Chaney's performance in *The Wolf Man* and remembered fondly

Lon Chaney, Jr. and Boris Karloff pose with serial actor William Desmond.

Lugosi's show-stopping turn as Ygor in *Son of Frankenstein*, a picture made at a time when, as new fathers, the artists found an unaccustomed bond.

Many of us who have grown up with these monsters, either in darkened movie palaces or via television or videocassette, have found a place in our hearts for the men who played Count Dracula, the Frankenstein Monster and the werewolf Larry Talbot.

The model kits—the toys—the posters—the magazines—the cartoon parodies—the character masks—the hit records, like John "The Cool Ghoul" Zacherley's "Dinner with Drac" and Bobby "Boris" Pickett's "Monster Mash"—all these and more would follow, cinching these portrayals as a celluloid Mount Rushmore of American pop mythology. We Americans like our mythological heroes and monsters to be the best of friends or the best of enemies. Being human, and being actors with egos, sometimes competing for the same class of role, Karloff, Lugosi and Chaney could be both.

A Monster Bash convention was held in 1997 at Ligonier, Pennsylvania, to honor the memory of Boris Karloff, Bela Lugosi and Lon Chaney, Jr. with an official unveiling of the U.S. Postal Service's mon-

"TRAPPED IN THE FLAMES"

Chapter 8

THE New UNIVERSAL presents

BELA LUGOSI
in
THE PHANTOM CREEPS

Robert KENT · Dorothy ARNOLD
Regis TOOMEY · Edward Van SLOAN

ster stamps, with the cooperation of the actors' heirs, Sara Karloff, Bela
G. Lugosi, Jr. and Ron Chaney. Bela Lugosi, Jr. suddenly called over to

Sara Karloff: "Hey! How come your Dad got two stamps, and my Dad only got one?" It was a question laced with humor, and with irony. Karloff's likeness from the 1932 version of *The Mummy* certainly belongs in the set, but Lugosi's fans would probably want Ygor from *Son of Frankenstein* in the set, too. Right after Lugosi, Jr.'s question, a fan yelled out, "Uh-oh! The feud's starting again!"

It was a funny remark, and it would be nice to think that somewhere, Bela, Sr., would get a laugh out of it as well.

The feature films and the very lives of Boris Karloff, Bela Lugosi and Lon Chaney, Jr. have been studied almost to excess, talked to death among the fans, and extensively chronicled. Yet the artists' serials have been given scant attention.

It is time we gave these neglected, misunderstood and underappreciated films their due. Certainly, the serials were intended primarily for children, but does that condition place them outside the realm of earnest scholarship? Should the works of Dr. Seuss and Lewis Carroll not be given the same attention as the works of Dickens and Shakespeare? Are the needs of children less important than the wants of adults? Purely rhetorical questions—the answers are patent.

And yes, the serials that Karloff, Lugosi and Chaney made—for the family-filmgoer trade, and then increasingly for a juvenile audience—deserve a place in history alongside *Frankenstein*, *Dracula* and *The Wolf Man*. For that matter, the serials are as vital a part of Hollywood's past as *Gone With the Wind*, *The Wizard of Oz* and *Casablanca*.

First, however, a spot of context: A look is in order at the history of the movie serial idiom as a class.

Sinister Serials

CHAPTER TWO
A Brief History of Movie Serials

"Children, it has always seemed to me, have a greater inherent understanding of many things than adults," Kinky Friedman writes in his novel, *Roadkill*, a crossbreed of whodunit mystery and homespun philosophical wisdom. "As they grow up, this native sensitivity is smothered, buried, and destroyed, like someone pouring concrete over cobblestones, and finally replaced by what we call knowledge." Knowledge, according to Albert Einstein, "is a vastly inferior commodity when compared with imagination. Imagination, of course, is the money of childhood. This is why it is no surprise that little children have a better understanding of Indians, nature, death, God, animals, the universe, and some truly hard to grasp concepts like the Catholic Church, than most adults."

Imagination is the very stuff of the movie serials. Serials gave children impossibly large heroes and heroines to admire, and colorful villains at whom to hiss and boo. Imagination, too, was the greater currency in which the serial-makers traded—the only currency that the studios' accounting offices could not pinch. The tight-fisted producers for whom directors like Ford Beebe, Sr. and Spencer Gordon Bennet worked encouraged—even ordered—these men to make reckless use of their imaginations in lieu of much time or much money. Somehow, the serials got made, usually within budget and schedule. Considering what little practical resources these men had to work with, it's amazing that their chapter plays kept kids queuing up at the box-office—and even more miraculous that a *Flash Gordon's Trip to Mars* or a *Superman* can still entertain audiences of the present day.

"The good serials—and there are some very good ones—more often than not survive on merits that we didn't even dream existed when we first saw them," as the film scholar William K. Everson once wrote. "To be enjoyed to the full, the serial had to be seen in those days paralleling our own days of innocence, when the movies truly had magic, when we truly believed everything that we saw on the screen, and when in our happy ignorance of critical standards or technical knowledge, the serial was judged by the same standards as a box-office blockbuster or an artistic masterpiece—and usually survived the comparison rather well."

Certainly, children nowadays are more sophisticated at a younger age than their parents or grandparents had been, but Everson's rule holds. A child may enjoy an episode of *Rugrats* on television as much as the latest Disney animated feature in a movie theater. If one likes the characters, and the story holds one's attention, it doesn't really matter if the show costs thousands or millions. Creative people still have to struggle fiercely against the cost-cutting fanatics.

From just before World War I to not long after the end of the Korean War (roughly, 1912 to 1956), many American youngsters went to their neighborhood movie theaters every Saturday—and wound up staying for almost an entire day. They went there to see a variety of short subjects along with the feature attraction, a cowboy picture, a mystery or a comedy. These short subjects might consist of cartoons, a newsreel, a comedy short (ancestor of the TV sitcom), a travelogue and previews of coming attractions. There would follow a feature film, or maybe a double or triple feature. More often than not, the audience also would watch a serial chapter.

Some theaters might show only cartoons for their kiddie matinees on any given Saturday, or only Westerns or horror films or comedies. There were second-run theaters that showed the big-budget films that had already played the large downtown theaters. Other theaters specialized in movies from years past. Large or small, downtown or right there in the neighborhood, all these theaters of bygone days fit the description of Movie Palace. The whole idea was to transplant the moviegoer out of the everyday routine into a place that was something special.

From the 1930s onward, if a serial was excitingly made, its studio could count on many, many kids (boys, in the majority) coming back week after week for three or four months at a stretch. Despite the fact that serials were part of the package that Saturday matinee crowds expected and were budgeted so that the studios would not lose money on them, the audiences expected some measure of quality. If a particular serial was above average or even merely good, there would almost always be a teaser following the end of that serial for the new serial that would start the next week. In some theaters, the manager would often run the first chapter of a new serial immediately following the end of the one that had occupied the past several weeks.

CHANDU ON THE MAGIC ISLAND

DISTRIBUTED BY PRINCIPAL DISTRIBUTING CORP

By the time television started to cause a drop in movie-theater attendance, beginning in the late 1940s, the studios began to make fewer and fewer films. Once the various craft unions had gained clout in Hollywood, it began to cost more to make movies. Furthermore, with the crumbling of the studio system, under which talents had signed long-term and often exclusive contracts, it no longer was possible to keep everyone on the payroll working steadily.

More so than any other studio, Republic Pictures considered its serials as important as any of its feature-film productions. The same crew members who labored on a self-contained picture would also put together a serial. While directors might want more time and money to produce a cliffhanger, what they had to work with at Republic in comparison to conditions at, say, the serial units of Universal or Columbia, made a difference for the better. Even the kids in the audience knew that Republic's serials were of a higher quality, as a rule, than those of the competition.

By the middle 1950s, Republic and Columbia stopped making serials altogether, since more kids were staying home to watch television.

As for television itself, such programs as *The Adventures of Superman* and *The Lone Ranger* were made by talents who had dealt in serials and Westerns.

"... [E]very once in a while, I watch one of the old serials on video, and you know what? They're still as much fun as they ever were: lively, fast-paced, imaginative—and sometimes downright strange," wrote Clayton Moore.

A movie serial—or cliffhanger, or chapter play—is an adventure story told in chapters. Each chapter barring the final one ends at some exciting point, where the conflict is at a peak.

Jon Tuska, in his serial history *The Vanishing Legion*, characterizes the chapter plays as dream-like. Indeed, at the most thrilling or frightening part of a dream, most dreamers wake up. The tensions in the dream go unresolved until the dream is analyzed, or one experiences the same dream to the point of making sense of it, or one dreams a resolution.

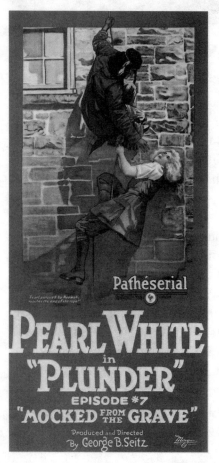

Pathéserial

Pearl pursued by Nemtok, reaches the end of the rope!

PEARL WHITE
in
"PLUNDER"
EPISODE #7
"MOCKED FROM THE GRAVE"
Produced and Directed
By George B. Seitz

Episodes of a novel are written so that the reader will want to immediately go to the next chapter, until the solution comes to light. This is the strategy of the movie serial, as well.

Movie serials have often been referred to as the movies' equivalent of comic strips. Comics, whose history parallels that of the cinema, probably are the most nearly cinematic of all printed art forms. Comic strips and movie serials are so similar in conception that it proves a foregone conclusion that some of the greatest movie serials would derive from comic-strip franchises.

From about the start of the World War I to the middle 1920s, the movie serials were considered a respectable form of entertainment, suitable for the entire family. Serial makers often catered to women: Responding to the rise of the Suffragette movement, and an increasing debate on the truer role of women in society, many of the early serials portrayed strong heroines. The most famous early serial is 1914's *The Perils of Pauline*, starring a rough-and-tumble Pearl White.

As the 1920s came to a close, the serial makers began aiming for a less sophisticated audience. The heyday of the talking-picture serial runs roughly from 1936 through 1942. We can credit this distinction to the kind of serials that Republic was making, serials that

looked more expensive than they actually were, with careful editing, slick photography and persuasive acting if not particularly fine writing. Universal's serials are a step below those of Republic in most fans' perception, but quite a few—in particular, the *Flash Gordon*s—are remembered with fondness.

Of the key serial studios, Universal dropped the idiom after 1946. Republic stopped producing serials in 1955, and Columbia axed its serial unit after 1956. Republic kept its serials in circulation, often under proxy titles. Some serials were sold outright to television producing companies.

Universal peddled much its serial inventory to companies like Goodwill Pictures and Filmcraft, which reissued the films theatrically. Other

SOL LESSER
presents

**BUSTER
CRABBE**

IN
A New EDGAR RICE
BURROUGHS Story

**"TARZAN
THE FEARLESS"**

ROMANCE!
THRILLS!
ADVENTURE!

with
JACQUELINE WELLS, EDWARD WOODS *and* A GREAT CAST

THE GREATEST TARZAN OF ALL TIME!

RELEASED BY PRINCIPAL DISTRIBUTING CORPORATION

Universals often turn up, with proxy main-title cards, from companies like Commonwealth Pictures, Film Classics and Serials, Inc. Crucial copyrights lapsed without the diligence of Universal's corporate machinery. Those Universal serials that were made under agreements with King Features Syndicate, including the trademark-bound *Flash Gordon*s, eventually reverted to the control of the syndicate, which leased them to television. Few Universal sound serials exist today in original form, and surviving public-domain prints in private collections are often poor copies. Some of the Universal serials appear lost, if not caught up in a maze of trademark-claim wrangling. Universal was about to merge with International Pictures and by the end of 1946 would cease serial production.

A number of Columbia's serials also have lapsed into the public domain, bereft of copyright, and oftentimes poorly made prints of these serials survive in private collections. The modern-day Columbia Pictures, however, does maintain some of the serials' master elements.

Columbia's *Batman* and *Superman* serials are now owned by Time-Warner, Inc., which has sporadically made them available on videocassette. But the trademark-holding successors of pulp-fiction publisher Harry Steger, who once licensed his *Spider* magazine proprietorship for two Columbia serials, have neglected to resurrect those films despite the occasional resurgence of *Spider* novels and comic books.

Overall, the Republic serials are in the best shape. This is due more to the vigilance of private collectors, however, than to any efforts on the part of the studio. But in more recent times, a company descended from Republic has restored the earlier films to near-authentic form.

Most of the silent and early talkie serials survive in fragmentary form. For such reasons, it is difficult to appraise this often-maligned genre of cinema with fairness.

A few serials (among them, 1933's *Tarzan the Fearless*) appear only to only exist in feature-length versions. These are serials cut down to a brisk clip of 60 to 100 minutes, made for the larger theaters that would not run serials or, later, for television. Oftentimes, a studio would release a feature version of a serial right around the time the serial was playing, but other cut-downs might surface years after the serial had played in its chapter-a-week form.

Some of the serials—despite changing tastes and the ravages of time—can still enthrall an audience. The wild, episodic plots are still studied and emulated by the likes of George Lucas and Steven Spielberg. Television series employ the cliffhanger tactics to keep their viewers tuning in, week after week. The serials are, in this practical sense, alive and well, thanks in part to serial stars Boris Karloff, Bela Lugosi and Lon Chaney, Jr.

Sinister Serials: Boris Karloff

CHAPTER THREE
The Gentlemanly Monster: The Sinister Serials of Boris Karloff

The conventional wisdom on Boris Karloff (1887-1969) holds that he patiently honed his craft in serials and small roles in feature films, then finally broke through in 1931's *Frankenstein*—and "never returned to the lowly chapter play," as the historian Roy Kinnard has put it. This is true enough, with or without the dash of opinion, and of course there is no accounting for taste as to the worth of the serial form in the greater scheme of cinema. Such a cavalier dismissal of the idiom is widespread, and its adherents neglect to consider that Karloff appeared in movies far less impressive than his known serial assignments. The enduring popularity of episodic television—weekly series, night-to-night miniseries and soap operas—proves the structural merits and narrative validity of the "lowly chapter play."

If Boris Karloff were still alive he would probably dismiss the study of his films and serials. Karloff never took himself too seriously as an actor and tended to downplay his earlier accomplishments when interviewed. Karloff would argue that his early years on the stage and then in motion pictures were nothing more than a training period to polish his skills and not worthy of the time of historians and fans. However, what survives of his serial work is worth more than a glance. His early role in *The Hope Diamond Mystery* allows the young actor to do some fine acting as a heroic character, a welcome change from the villains he usually portrayed.

Serials in the early 1920s we still considered prestige family entertainment. By the time Karloff would appear in *King of the Wild*, 10 years later, the serial audience was composed mainly of children. Karloff saw little merit in these parts and either hammed it up or did only what the director required. Serial making, as Karloff well knew, was difficult work and Karloff worked as hard as any cast and crew on his serials, although the spark he became known for was missing.

Such old-time serial directors as Ford Beebe, Spencer Gordon Bennet, Ray Taylor, William Witney and John English would have relished the more generous budgets and expanded time for preparation that their teleseries counterparts enjoy today. But then again, Mark Frost has often cited the near impossibility of producing his and David Lynch's serial-for-television, *Twin Peaks*, in light of time-and-money crunches. Television stars Dennis Franz and George Clooney have plenty in common with Buster Crabbe and Clayton Moore. It all stems from the shared responsibility, in one generation or another, of carrying a chapter-a-week continuing adventure, and from the shared burden of typecasting despite ambitions to broaden their popular identification beyond serialized entertainment.

More than just a touchstone of our cultural heritage, the big-screen serial retains relevance beyond its foreshadowing of episodic television. Some are interesting as antiques, and some are downright enthralling as fantasy-laden escapism. Nor is the perceived "lowliness" of the serials a new consideration: Director Ed Bernds once noted that the industry considered the talents involved with Columbia's serial unit to be unemployable in other sectors. Even the artists responsible for Columbia's short comedies—including the *Three Stooges* series, on which Bernds worked—were accorded more respect than the serial-makers. Time has, of course, proved the snobs wrong, for the better *Stooges* shorts and the few genuinely watchable Columbia serials are still popularly well received.

The serials that have withstood the test of time have done so in spite of the conditions under which they were made. Long, grueling hours of shooting were never enough to overcome the tight-schedule treadmill that seldom allowed rewrites, re-shoots or even rehearsals. Directors William Witney and John English could take pride in *Drums of Fu Manchu* (1940) and *Adventures of Captain Marvel* (1941); or Ray Taylor in *Gordon of Ghost City* (1933); or Ford Beebe and Robert F. Hill in *Flash Gordon's Trip to Mars* (1938). But theirs was a clandestine, guerrilla pride, born of artistic success despite pinched finances and hurried schedules, and quite unlike the pride David O. Selznick might take in one of his company's well-heeled, leisurely productions. It is almost miraculous that the Spencer Gordon Bennet/Thomas Carr *Superman* (1948) came

Adventures of CAPTAIN MARVEL

Based on the character in
WHIZ COMICS Magazine

A **REPUBLIC** SERIAL
IN **12** CHAPTERS

TOM TYLER
FRANK COGHLAN, JR.
WILLIAM BENEDICT · LOUISE CURRIE
WILLIAM WITNEY and JOHN ENGLISH
Directors

off as well as it did, given the pinchpenny essence of Sam Katzman's Columbia unit. Ford Beebe, Jr. has mentioned that his father would undertake rewrites and camera set-up plans while off the studio clock, putting in 18-hour days.

One of the elder Beebe's major disappointments was the first million-dollar serial production, *Riders of Death Valley* (1941); co-directed with Ray Taylor. Universal Pictures' big-ticket investment went more toward promotional hype and name-brand casting—Dick Foran, Leo Carillo, Buck Jones, Charles Bickford, Big Boy Williams, Noah Beery, Jr. and Lon Chaney, Jr.—than toward the filmmaking art. Stock footage abounds, and the chronic doubling of Rod Cameron for Jones becomes an embarrassment. Denied crucial time to rework the script or achieve original spectacle, Beebe found the project a chore that might as well have been produced in the customary six-digit budgetary range.

Karloff's villainous Arab, Mustapha, is arrested in this scene from *King of the Wild* **(1931).**

Boris Karloff most likely would not have wanted to tackle another serial after 1931's *King of the Wild*. But if he ever placed his serials in perspective with the tedious *Frankenstein 1970* (1958) or the opulent but boring *The Climax* (1944), he might have longed to swap either of those features for another chapter-play turn.

History generally holds that Karloff made five or six serials during his long trudge toward stardom. He actually may have made nine or 10, if not more. The problem in accounting for Karloff's early span is that he himself neglected to document the array of roles, small and large, that he played before the breakout. The very chemistry and technology of film-making, too, works against documentation: Natural decomposition occurred alarmingly early, and many pictures were destroyed for the sake of reclaiming the silver in the nitrate film stock. Not only do many pioneering companies no longer exist, but neither do their files of production and personnel.

Of the better-documented serials that Karloff graced, only three exist intact: *The Hope Diamond Mystery* (1921), *King of the Wild* (1931) and *The Vanishing Legion* (1931). A somewhat more elusive *King of the Kongo*

Sinister Serials: Boris Karloff

(1929)—the first sound serial, from Nat Levine's Mascot Pictures—was released as a silent, as a silent-with-music version including synchronized accompaniment on Victor Talking Machine discs, and as a part-talking version with sound-on-disc. Apparently, only a sound version survives, but without its original audio discs. Historian Wayne Schutz maintains that the discs may exist in England, possibly at the British Film Institute or at America's Library of Congress. An exhaustive search at the Library of Congress has turned up numerous discs, catalogued only by manufacturers' matrix and serial numbers without reference to any titles. The *King of the Kongo* originals may well repose among these nameless platters.

Karloff's name also crops up in light of a phonetically confusing trio of serials: *The Lightning Raider* (1918), *The Masked Rider* (1919) and *The Vanishing Rider* (1928). The absence of screen credits for Karloff, or even a mention in the publicity materials, suggests small roles—if any at all. Karloff had yet to make a mark as a screen actor in 1918-19 and would likely have served *Lightning* and *Masked* as an extra.

"Nobody knew I was in Hollywood for 10 years," Karloff said in a late-in-life interview with radio announcer Colin Edwards, "except me and the landlady to whom I was covertly owing rent." Karloff's persistence had by 1928, however, made him a known dependable, and he probably carried at least a small role in *The Vanishing Rider*. In any event, *The Lightning Raider*, *The Masked Rider* and *The Vanishing Rider* are mislaid if not lost outright, and their absence balks the search for the most telling clue: Karloff's own distinctive aspect. These titles' presence in any Karloff filmography can only be taken on faith. Meanwhile, the historian Jim Stringham has found an actor who looks strikingly like Karloff in a still from an American-made *Fantomas* serial (Fox; 1921).

Beverly Bare Buehrer's 1993 book, *Boris Karloff: A Bio-Bibliography*, begins the Karloff checklist with *His Majesty the American* (1919). The Buehrer roster takes a "cannot be confirmed" stance as to Karloff's participation in *The Dumb Girl of Portici* (1916) and the serials *The Lightning Raider* and *The Masked Rider*. Karloff, in his later years, often cited *His Majesty the American* as his launching point, as a crowd extra. A family friend, Cynthia Lindsay, in her 1975 biography *Dear Boris: The Life of William Henry Pratt a.k.a. Boris Karloff*, lists *Portici*, along with *Lightning* and *Masked*—and so does latter-day Karloff biographer Scott Allen Nollen. Four chapters, as yet unrestored, from *Lightning* have come late to light at Ottowa's National Film, Television & Sound Archives and the UCLA Film & Television Archives, but are unavailable for screening at this time. Against the day the lost and fragmentary serials might bear a deep screening (and unlikelier things have happened) to prove the filmographies right or wrong, a discussion of the Karloff serials must begin with the presumption of his work in *The Lightning Raider*.

THE LIGHTNING RAIDER
(Pathé; 1918-19)

The Lightning Raider fits in among the over 90 percent of historic world cinema considered lost or incomplete. Pathé was tops in the serial field, even to the point of brandishing the slogan, "The House of Serials." George B. Seitz was among Pathé's front-rank directors at the time; he is better remembered today for his work on the *Andy Hardy* series, starring Mickey Rooney, at MGM during the 1930s and '40s. Spencer Gordon Bennet, a serial stuntman and later a director in his own right, worked with Seitz in the early days. It is possible that Bennet participated without credit in some capacity on this serial, for his daughter, Harriet Pessis, has said Bennet learned much about directing from Seitz. Seitz was an accomplished hand at in-the-camera editing, a natural talent that allowed him to pace and photograph a scene much as it would look in the final presentation.

Screenwriter Bertram Millhauser enjoyed a long career. Over a generation later, Millhauser was still plugging away on Universal's *Sherlock Holmes* series, and later yet he contributed to early-day television's *Lone Ranger* series.

The Lightning Raider also boasts a fascinating cast: Pearl White had become world-famous in the few years since *The Perils of Pauline* (Pathé; 1914). In a set of notes prepared for his daughter, Bennet recalled Miss White as "an all-around 'regular guy,'" and she offered anyone five dollars to catch her with a cigarette, when she was trying to give up smoking." Warner Oland was already well established as a $1,000-a-week actor in those pre-Charlie Chan days—and already associated with Oriental roles, though of a villainous stripe. It is interesting that, after *The Lightning Raider*, both Oland and Karloff would impersonate Sax Rohmer's Chinese conqueror, Dr. Fu Manchu, and that they would eventually meet again on camera in 1936's *Charlie Chan at the Opera*. Of course, the caste distinctions between the star player Oland and the likely extra Karloff would have made their work on *Lightning* something less than a collaboration.

The story—synopsized from chapter summaries provided by the historian Jim Stringham—finds "the cleverest girl thief in the world" (Miss White) romancing millionaire Thomas Norton (Henry Gsell) while plotting the downfall of her mortal enemy, Wu Fang (Oland). The Raider outwits Wu Fang at almost every turn, with the help of an eccentric menace called the Wasp (William Burt). At one point, Wu thwarts the Raider's plan to marry Norton by convincing them that they are brother and sister. Wu's own romance ends badly. Finally, a mortally wounded Wu Fang confesses all—out of tradition, not remorse—and the Raider and Norton are married before an assemblage of reformed crooks.

Recent research by serial historians has confirmed that Chapters 6, 11 and possibly Chapter 14 exist in Ottawa. Historian Wayne Schutz has

Pearl White's heroine is saved from the villainy of Wang Fu (Warner Oland) in ***The Lightning Raider.*** **(Photofest)**

Pearl White and Warner Oland in *The Lightning Raider*. (Photofest)

been told that a fragment of an untitled chapter exists at UCLA's Film and Television Archives. According to historians Eric Stedman and Henry Miyamoto, the Library of Congress has Chapters 2, 3, 8, 13 and 14 in their collection. Hopefully before long we will finally learn if Karloff appeared in this serial or was lost on the cutting room floor.

Fragmentary reviews are almost as elusive as the film itself. The show business tradepapers were more concerned with box-office potential than with aesthetic considerations, and seldom would critique a serial from start to finish. In a favorable take on *Lightning*'s Chapter No. 4, "Through Doors of Steel," *Moving Picture World* cited "both novelty and surprise." A later dispatch in the *World* raved that "Pathé has [*The Lightning Raider*] in practically every available theater open to serials in the New York territory."

CREDITS: Director: George B. Seitz; Screenplay: Bertram Millhauser and George B. Seitz; a Serial in 15 Chapters; Released: January 5, 1919,

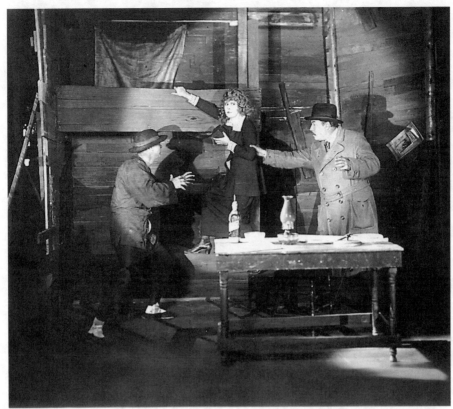

Serial queen Pearl White faces more adventures in *The Lightning Raider*. (Photofest)

by Pathé Exchange (Biographer Scott Allen Nollen cites a mid-December 1918 release)

CAST: Pearl White (The Lightning Raider); Henry Gsell [in some sources, Henry G. Sell] (Thomas Norton); Warner Oland (Wu Fang); Frank Redman (Hop Sing); William Burt (The Wasp); Nellie Burt (Sunbeam); Ruby Hoffman (Lottie); and Sam Kim, Henrietta Simpson, William A. Sullivan, Anita Brown and [presumably] Boris Karloff

CHAPTER TITLES: 1) "The Ebony Block"; 2) "The Counterplot"; 3) "Underworld Terrors"; 4) "Through Doors of Steel"; 5) "The Brass Key"; 6) "The Mystic Box"; 7) "Meshes of Evil"; 8) "Cave of Dread"; 9) "Falsely Accused"; 10) "The Baited Trap"; 11) "The Bars of Death"; 12) "Hurled Into Space"; 13) "The White Roses"; 14) "Cleared of Guilt"; 15) "Wu Fang Atones"

WILLIAM STEINER

presents

The Fifteen Episode Western Serial

"The MASKED RIDER"

Written and Directed by AUBREY M. KENNED'

Featuring

RUTH STONEHOUSE,
PAUL PANZER
and HARRY MYERS

Episode No. 4

"THE KISS OF HATE"

Distributed by ARROW

THE MASKED RIDER
(Arrow Pictures; 1919)

This entry from a long-defunct rival to Pathé marks what would appear to be Boris Karloff's second serial assignment. The serial-conscious Arrow Pictures was among innumerable studios that collapsed before the advent of talking pictures. Harry C. Myers is probably best known to movie buffs as the drunken millionaire playboy in Charles Chaplin's *City Lights* (1931). In *The Masked Rider*, Myers plays Harry Burrell, the hero. Paul Panzer, the dastardly villain of *The Perils of Pauline* (1914), plays another slimy character, known as Pancho, in this entry. Leading lady Ruth Stonehouse was one of many contenders for Pearl White's high station. Karloff's participation is open to speculation.

So, too, is speculation called for as to the very nature of the film beyond a frontier setting. A surviving fragmentary press kit stresses the mystery of whether the Masked Rider is a man or a woman. Women had a better chance of playing the hero—or the antihero, as in *The Lightning Raider*—in those proto-feminist Suffragette days. But then, barely a generation later the notion of a lady-to-the-rescue character would seem a novelty, as exploited in 1939's *Daredevils of the Red Circle*. The pressbook also crows about a spectacle involving "over 10,000 steers," which sounds quite unlike anything in which the notoriously cheap and decidedly unspectacular producer, William Steiner, would have indulged.

CREDITS: Producer: William Steiner; Director and Scenarist: Aubrey M. Kennedy; a Serial in 15 Chapters; Released: May 1919

CAST: Harry Myers (Harry Burrell); Ruth Stonehouse (Ruth Chadwick); Paul Panzer (Pancho); Edna M. Holland (Juanita); Marie Toreador [given elsewhere as Marie Treador] ("Ma" Chadwick); Blanche Gillespie (Blanche); Robert Tiber, (Santaz); Jack Chapman (Captain Jack); and George Murdock, George Cravey and [presumably] Boris Karloff

CHAPTER TITLES: 1) "The Hole in the Wall"; 2) "In the Hands of Pancho"; 3) "The Capture of Juanita"; 4) "The Kiss of Hate"; 5) "The Death Trap"; 6) "Pancho Plans Revenge"; 7) "The Fight on the Dam"; 8) "The Conspirators Foiled"; 9) "The Exchange of Prisoners"; 10) "Harry's Perilous Leap"; 11) "To the Rescue"; 12) "The Imposter"; 13) "Coals of Fire"; 14) "In the Desert's Grip"; 15) "Retribution"

FANTOMAS
(Fox Film Corp.; 1920-21)

Valuable pointers in what seems the right direction have come from Wayne Schutz (who mentioned it) and Jim Stringham (who provided persuasive documentation). It seems likelier than ever before that Boris Karloff handled a role in this American remake of a popular French "continuing adventure" photoplay.

The evidence is slim—only a photograph, and an artist's rendering of the same scene for a poster. A gentleman at left, wearing a hat and a mustache, restraining a character who might be a butler, looks amazingly like Karloff. A typewritten legend on the back of the photo reads: "FANTOMAS (Fox; 1920 [*sic*] serial) Boris Karloff, Edna Murphy." And yes, the leading lady-of-record *is* Edna Murphy.

Publicity materials make it abundantly clear that the serial required 20 episodes instead of the customary 15. Only a fragmentary synopsis is possible just now, owing to equally fragmentary press kits and the missing state of the film itself. Super-criminal Fantomas (Edward Roseman) comes to America and decides to retire. If the law will pardon him, he promises, he will become a model citizen. The police demand unconditional surrender. Angered, Fantomas announces that he will kidnap prominent scientist James D. Harrington (Lionel Adams) "under the very noses of the police force" and announces the moment at which he will perform the abduction. Detective Fred Dixon (John Willard) plots a capture. Harrington, abducted, proves to have developed a formula for processing gold but intends to destroy it because of the economic chaos such a development would cause. Fantomas plots to possess the formula and incidentally falls in love with the professor's daughter, Ruth (Edna Murphy). Fred, Ruth and her sweetheart, Jack Meredith (Johnnie Walker) try to stop Fantomas. "What would you do," asks the pressbook, "if you were a girl... and one of the most daring criminals in the world had you in his power so that unless you married him, your father and your sweetheart would die! What would you do?"

A character called "the Woman in Black" appears to be a rejected wife or lover of Fantomas, inevitably to be involved in the villain's downfall. She will help Ruth only insofar as she can have Fantomas to herself;

From the Americanized *Fantomas*. Can the mustachioed character be anyone other than Boris Karloff?

otherwise, she takes the thief's side. This touch is typical of the earlier serials, whose romantic complications helped to sustain the extended running time without narrative padding. When serials later came to be aimed at ever-younger audiences, such subplotting disappeared—with notable exceptions, including 1936's *Flash Gordon*. *Fantomas* leaves a decoy captive to the mercies of the police; springs a firetrap on the heroes; places Ruth in the villain's clutches and confronts her with a "Wild Man"; and threatens the professor with torture—among other sadistic delights.

The player best known to modern-day viewers is Henry Armetta, as a henchman. Armetta later would register as a comical supporting actor, notably in the Laurel and Hardy feature *Fra Diavolo* (1933). Director

Edward Sedgwick, a former Texas lawman during the Mexican Revolution, later became a comedy specialist at MGM. Sedgwick directed early footage for the 1925 *The Phantom of the Opera*, only to be replaced by Rupert Julien. It seems likely that Karloff's role is that of a member of Fantomas' gang. Actor Johnnie Walker was well known in his day, and he would again play a heroic part in a serial opposite Karloff, the evidently lost *Vultures of the Sea* (1928).

The serial idiom was at its peak of respectability during the early 1920s. William Fox's big studio would cease making serials as the 1920s rolled on, but would keep a hand in the idiom via independent producer Sol Lesser (see *The Return of Chandu*, in the chapter on Bela Lugosi's work). *Fantomas* garnered a mixed response from theater managers, as accounted for in a recurring feature called *What the Picture Did for Me* in the tradepaper *Exhibitor's Herald*. "The Italians... are packing the house at every episode," wrote an ethnicity-conscious Brooklyn operator. "It is just an average serial," reported Brownsville, Texas' Dreamland Theatre. And Knoxville, Tennessee's Gem Theatre raved, "On sixth episode and holding up good."

CREDITS: Producer: William Fox; Director and Scenarist: Edward Sedgwick; Based upon the Novels of Marcél Allain and Pierre Souvéstre; Photographed by: Horace Plympton; a Serial in 20 Chapters; Released: December 19, 1920 [Publicity materials cite a 1921 release]

CAST: Edward Roseman (Fantomas); Edna Murphy (Ruth Harrington); Lionel Adams (James D. Harrington); Johnnie Walker (Jack Meredith); John Willard (Fred Dixon); Eve Belfour (Woman in Black); Irving Brooks (Duke); Ben Walker (Butler); Henry Armetta ("Wop"); Rena Parker (Countess); and to all appearances, Boris Karloff

CHAPTER TITLES: 1) "On the Stroke of Nine"; 2) "The Million-Dollar Reward"; 3) "The Triple Peril"; 4) "Blades of Terror"; 5) "Heights of Horror"; 6) "The Altar of Sacrifice"; 7) "Flames of Destruction"; 8) "At Death's Door"; 9) "The Haunted Hotel"; 10) "The Fatal Card"; 11) "The Phantom Sword"; 12) "The Danger Signal"; 13) "On the Count of Three"; 14) "The Blazing Train"; 15) "The Sacred Necklace"; 16) "The Phantom Shadow"; 17) "The Price of Fang Wu"; 18) "Double-Crossed"; 19) "The Hawk's Prey"; 20) "The Hell Ship"

THE HOPE DIAMOND MYSTERY
(Kosmik Films; 1921)

The credits on *The Hope Diamond Mystery* identify writer May Yohe as "the former Lady Frances Hope" and claim a basis in her memoirs. Each end title, announcing the forthcoming chapter, is signed by May Yohe. The serial is, of course, more fiction than fact. (More later on the bizarre truth of the Hope Diamond.) Dame Yohe was a figure of some celebrity, probably more for the fact of who she was than for any literary gifts; the first few episodes show her seated at a desk, writing in a journal, as if revealing the story on the spot. The more substantial writing, of course, came from scenarists Charles Goddard, of *The Perils of Pauline* screenplay, and John B. Clymer.

Existing only in archival form at this writing, *The Hope Diamond Mystery* proves to be a gem, with an exceptionally fine performance by Karloff. A chapter-by-chapter synopsis follows:

Chapter No. 1: "The Hope Diamond Mystery" begins with May Yohe's baleful words: "...Lives and loves down through the centuries lay as wasted, wrecked things in the cruel wake of that Diamond, menacing in its lurid gleam as the very eye of Lucifer the Fallen..." Karloff crops up as a 16th-century Hindu priest, guarding the diamond as an ornament on a sacred statue. The diamond is stolen. Karloff pronounces a curse, in a broad foreshadowing of his showy star turn in 1932's *The Mummy*. Cut to the early 1920s, and we find Lord Francis Hale (Captain C. Clayton) considering buying the Hope Diamond from his friend, James Marcon (William Marion), a broker from New York. Marcon demands an astounding £48,000.

Boris Karloff shows up as the mysterious Dakar, all decked out in turban and stylish mustache. We meet Reginald Travers (William Buckley), a supposed friend who has been trifling with Lord Hale's wife (Ethel Shannon). Watching the house is a neighbor, Sydney Atherton (Harry Carter), who is secretly known as Nang Fu, a master criminal. (Harry Carter resembles a cross between Warner Oland and Bela Lugosi.) Atherton's servant, Saki (Frank Seka), observes the goings-on while hiding.

Lady Hale wants to wear the diamond before deciding whether she wants to own it. Dakar shadows Lady Hale, but Atherton believes Marcon has taken the gem to his hotel. Atherton sends a thug to steal the jewel. The bandit threatens Marcon, who apparently is shot as he hesitates.

Chapter No. 2: "The Vanishing Hand" begins as we meet the hero, amateur criminologist John Gregge (George Chesebro), and Mary Hilton (Grace Darmond), Marcon's secretary. Meanwhile, Dakar visits Marcon's hotel, where he finds the man apparently dead. Atherton/Nang Fu has discovered that Marcon did not have the diamond, and has sent his thugs to take the stone from Lady Hale. Mary Hilton discovers Nang Fu in the house and sees the diamond, which has been quickly slipped into a wineglass. She reaches for the glass as the lights go out, and someone shoots at her.

Chapter No. 3: "The Forged Note" starts with the information that James Marcon is in a state of shock. Dakar attempts to reclaim the diamond by forging a note in Marcon's name. Atherton takes the bait and heads back toward Marcon's hotel. A hotel detective halts Atherton's contingent. The villains overpower the detective and forge a note of their own, declaring that Marcon has decided not to sell the diamond.

Lord Hale now has two conflicting forgeries. The police have recovered the diamond from a mailbox—placed there when Mary Hilton and Atherton's accomplice were fighting as the lights went out. Lord Hale calls on Scotland Yard. Hale also discovers that his wife has been unfaithful. Gregge and Mary, meanwhile, have been trying to reach Marcon and head for Lord Hale's manor. Dakar, seeing the Scotland Yard inspectors approaching, grabs the diamond and escapes by leaping from a bridge into the river.

Chapter No. 4: "The Jewel of Sita" finds Gregge and Mary catching up with Dakar, who has taken refuge aboard a houseboat. Dakar is far from the menacing sort he appears to be. He has taken the diamond to return it to the sacred statue of Sita in India. A theme of reincarnation is subtly introduced here, as Dakar is characterized as "the man of a thousand memories." Dakar is dripping wet and miserably cold from his plunge, but he enchants Gregge and Mary—who we now learn are really detectives in Marcon's employ—with the story of the accursed diamond. Karloff's expressive eyes and knowing face are just right for this sequence; he does more subtly effective acting here than any volume of sweeping theatrical gestures would have conveyed.

Now, James Marcon appears to have been killed by Atherton's henchmen, and Travers has been shot and killed by the fleeing Atherton. Lady Hale has left her husband, and is carrying on with one Putnam Bradley Stone. Of all the serials covered here, *The Hope Diamond Mystery* is the most like a present-day television soap opera, and it shows the serial-makers were still hoping to pull a broader audience than just the juvenile trade.

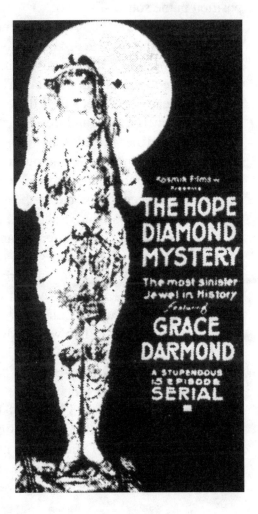

Most of this chapter concerns itself with Dakar, Gregge and Mary, and with the flashback sequence. In 16th-century India, we meet the boisterous adventurer Jean Baptiste Tavanier (Chesebro). He falls in love with the beautiful Bibi (Grace Darmond), one of the ceremonial virgins in a temple. Bibi's father, Bagi (William Marion) is a miser, "willing to sell the happiness of the daughter, Bibi, to the highest bidder." Karloff plays the high priest in a magnificent temple "set. Ghung (Harry Carter), a rich trader, lusts after Bibi, and Bagi is more than willing to make a deal with him. Bibi is forbidden to see Tavanier. Even though it is forbidden for an infidel to enter the temple, Tavanier sneaks in; but Ghung's spies catch him and a riot breaks out.

Chapter No. 5: "A Virgin's Love" begins with Tavanier being chased out of the temple. Ghung stirs up the villagers against Tavanier, who escapes. Bagi pleads with his daughter to marry Ghung, but she refuses. One of Ghung's spies ransacks Tavanier's baggage and plants within it a scorpion. Tavanier arrives at Bagi's home and states that he will offer his treasures for the right to marry Bibi. Bagi agrees. Tavanier's servant opens the chest and is stung fatally by the scorpion. Ghung's spy, disappointed to have killed the wrong victim, lunges at Tavanier with a knife. (This section of an archival safety-film print betrays significant nitrate decomposition in the source-film stock.)

Chapter No. 6: "The House of Terror" resumes with the struggle. Tavanier kills the spy. He discovers his money has been stolen. Desperate, Tavanier ponders the ease of stealing the diamond from the statue. Bagi experiences a vision of Sita. (The double-exposure effect of the statue's appearance is very well done, given the time and the technology.) Frightened, Bagi implores Bibi to devote her life to the temple. Bibi, convinced that Tavanier has been killed, tearfully consents. Tavanier steals cautiously toward the religious icon. Bibi is overjoyed to see him— but not at all happy about his trying to steal the jewel. Tavanier seems to be won over by her appeal, but as she agrees to leave with him, Tavanier secretly takes the diamond. Suddenly, a huge cloud of smoke erupts as an alarm, and lions are sent after Tavanier.

Karloff, as the priest, lunges at Tavanier. In self-defense, Tavanier wounds the priest. While dying, the priest invokes a curse upon Tavanier until the diamond is restored. A lion attacks Tavanier, but he kills it. Tavanier, escaping, sells the diamond. Tavanier disguises himself as an East Indian and plans to flee with Bibi. But Ghung has planted another spy, in the guise of a beggar. While Tavanier prepares for the journey, Ghung's accomplices kidnap Bibi and demand to know where Tavanier's loot is hidden.

Chapter No. 7: "The Flames of Despair" begins as Ghung pretends to attack the spies threatening Bibi. Ghung seeks to convince Bibi that the spies work for Tavanier, and he implies that Tavanier has been unworthy of her. This confuses Bibi, especially as she has discovered that Tavanier had stolen the sacred jewel. Ghung asks her again to marry him. Not knowing what else to do, she consents. Ghung playfully teases her father with his payment of a bag of gold as Bibi's dowry, and fantasizes about making love to Bibi. But there is another woman in the villainous Ghung's life: Mizra, a possessive dancer (played by Carmen Phillips). Ghung is flattered by Mizra's jealousy—until he discovers that she has poisoned a glass of wine meant for Bibi.

One of Ghung's servants attacks Bagi as he is about to hide

Grace Darmond, as Mary Hilton, survives a shipwreck toward the end of *The Hope Diamond Mystery*.

the gold. Tavanier overpowers the thief. As he lay dying Bagi reveals to Tavanier the pact with Ghung for Bibi's marriage. Bibi repents as she finds herself repulsed by Ghung's lustful advances. Tavanier, hearing Bibi's screams, attacks Ghung. Bibi eascapes and finds her dying father, who asks her forgiveness.

Meanwhile, Mizra kills Ghung, rescuing Tavanier. Ghung is cremated to appease the gods. Bibi allows herself to be sacrificed for her sins. Tavanier, we learn from a title card, is "torn to death by wild dogs."

Chapter No. 8: "Yellow Whisperings" flashes forward to modern times. Marcon is alive. Dakar has somehow restored him from "a strange condition of suspended animation" which Nang Fu, aka Sidney Atherton, has caused. Dakar has killed one of Nang Fu's henchmen, and has restored the accursed jewel to Marcon. Marcon, in fact, is frightened yet fascinated by the gem. Marcon begins to distrust Mary and Gregge, along with everyone else around him. Nang Fu has been sending Marcon death threats; and Marcon is convinced that in every shadow, Nang Fu is waiting for him. We also learn that Mary Hilton is susceptible to hypnosis, and that at times Sydney Atherton has secretly hypnotized her. Atherton believes that she can lead him to the diamond.

At midnight, Nang Fu's men invade Marcon's hotel room. Mary's hypnotic spell fades, and she declines to steal the diamond. Nang Fu, furious at the botched attempt, threatens Mary. Gregge pounds on the locked door.

Here we find striking evidence of the sloppiness that plagues many serials. Problems in plot construction grew when multiple writers worked on a script, and a glitch in one writer's text may not have been noticed until too late. How could James Marcon be in a state of suspended animation? Did he have a seizure, or was he drugged or hypnotized? This device is never explained.

Chapter No. 9: "The Evil Eye" is fascinating for its explicit presaging of a scene from Bela Lugosi's starring picture of 1932, *White Zombie*—just one more ironic bit of history to enhance the Karloff-Lugosi mystique. About which, more in a moment.

John Gregge breaks open the door, grabs Mary and escapes to Marcon's room. Nang Fu, however, finds Mary after John leaves. Nang Fu demands that Mary tell him what has become of the diamond. Frightened, Mary tells Nang Fu that John has the diamond. Nang Fu suspects that Mary is lying—he believes the jewel reposes in a trunk in Marcon's room. Nang Fu and his henchmen carry the trunk out to search it. Nang Fu climbs to the roof to confront John Gregge. The men, embroiled in a fight, are spotted by the police. The policemen overpower most of the Chinese villains and then search for Nang Fu. Meanwhile, Marcon has staged a fake robbery, leaving the safe open during all the confusion. Marcon now hopes that Nang Fu and the other miscreants will believe someone else has stolen the diamond. But Nang Fu has been watching Marcon. He waits in hiding.

Watching Mary through her window, Nang Fu waits for her to turn and see him. Nang Fu stares at her, Dracula-like, and hypnotizes her. He tells her to pick up a knife and kill the sleeping John Gregge, stationed at her doorway. Mary is about to kill John, but then a hand dashes the knife away.

The scenes involving hypnosis—the close-ups of Nang Fu's eyes, the cutting to show Mary's face, the way she holds the knife—seem fa-

Boris Karloff and Captain C. Clayton in *The Hope Diamond Mystery*.

miliar. Finally comes the hand, intervening in the nick of time. This scene would be virtually duplicated just over a decade later in *White Zombie*.

Chapter No. 10: "In the Spider's Web" starts out with the hand dislodging the knife from Mary's grasp. The person who intervenes is Dakar. Nang Fu appears to Dakar as a menacing vision. (There are echoes here of yet another Lugosi film, the 1934 serial *The Return of Chandu*, in which Lugosi's title character represents a mysterious figure fighting for good causes, much like Karloff's Dakar.) Dakar cannot break Mary's trance or prevent her from answering a summons from the villain.

Dakar finds a note given to Mary and shares the information with John. A policeman plans to have Mary followed. Dakar, not wanting the detective to know of Mary's involvement with Nang Fu, knocks the lawman unconscious. Meanwhile, John discovers Nang Fu's hideout, only to be captured. John is relieved to see Mary brought into the room, although she remains mesmerized. Nang Fu questions Mary about the diamond, and Mary infuriates him by stating that it was stolen. John is locked up and cannot rescue Mary.

The film achieves considerable spectacle here on what can only have been a modest budget. The sliding walls that trap John Gregge are a formidable job of set-building.

Chapter No. 11: "The Cup of Fear" begins with an introduction to the jealous Wanda, wife of Sydney Atherton (aka Nang Fu). Meanwhile, John can no longer abide hearing Mary's screams, so he lies to Nang Fu—telling him he knows where the diamond is hidden. Nang Fu forces John and Mary to wear rings that will emit a poison. If John tells the truth, he and Mary will be given an antidote. If John is lying, they will die.

James Marcon has a detective pose as a butler for a dinner party. Sydney Atherton, dropping the Nang Fu get-up, and his wife cunningly have themselves invited, and John and Mary are among the guests. Atherton is amused, for the couple can do nothing against him as long as they are wearing the poison rings, which of course they cannot remove. Blaine has the police standing by. A phone call from one of Nang Fu's men tells Marcon to watch Dakar closely. Atherton declares that his wine tastes funny just as Mary is about to drink. Mary looks at Atherton and suddenly realizes that he is Nang Fu. It looks as though the poison is taking effect on Mary.

Chapter No. 12: "The Ring of Death" begins with Atherton's manipulations of Marcon. Disguised as Nang Fu, Atherton makes a search. The police find Marcon, apparently slain. Atherton, back in civilian guise, staggers into the room and accuses the now-missing Dakar. Atherton informs John and Mary that he has destroyed the antidote.

Chapter No. 13: "The Lash of Hate" reveals that Dakar has found an antidote, which he leaves in a vial. In a note, Dakar reveals that he possesses the Hope Diamond and instructs the couple to meet him at the houseboat. Saki (Frank Seka), one of Nang Fu's gang, leads a party to capture John, Mary and Dakar.

Wanda Atherton, sensing that her evil husband lusts after Mary, plans to do away with the girl. Aboard his yacht, Atherton orders the captives to change into more fitting seagoing attire, so that he can search their clothing. Nothing is found. Atherton decides to torture them. John suffers a beating. The yacht's captain protests Wanda's plans for Mary. Atherton knocks the captain unconscious. The captives endure days of torture, but no one talks. Wanda is disgusted with Atherton's failure, saying: "Maybe the girl's eyes are brighter to you than the diamond."

First Mate Johnson (Harry Archer) helps Mary, John and Dakar escape. Mary has apparently been spared a beating. Wanda demands that her husband make Mary talk. Atherton, drinking heavily, agrees. He discovers that his prisoners and Johnson have escaped—and also set fire to the yacht. The yacht blows up in a poorly executed miniature effect. John, Mary, Dakar and Johnson swim to an island. Sydney and Wanda Atherton have survived the explosion and reached the island.

Chapter No. 14: "Primitive Passions" finds Dakar, Johnson, John and Mary washed up on the beach. It takes them a while to find each other; Atherton's crewmen discover the fugitives. An accomplice learns that Dakar has the diamond. Johnson intervenes, and the crewman falls from a cliff. He survives, however, and tells the Athertons of the diamond and the former captives' presence. Atherton declares that nothing will stop him now, but his wife says that she will take care of the matter.

John and Dakar leave Mary to search for food. Atherton's crewmen discover Johnson. Atherton orders him beaten until he tells where the others are hiding. Meanwhile, Wanda Atherton pretends to lie unconscious on the shore. She fools everyone but Dakar. Wanda suddenly lunges at Mary with a knife.

Chapter No. 15: "An Island of Destiny" begins with a struggle between the women. Wanda stabs John as he and Dakar come to Mary's rescue. The men break up the fight, but Wanda escapes. Johnson escapes his captors. When Wanda returns, beaten and empty-handed, Atherton sneers at her failure. Something in her attitude disturbs him however: "Damn you, you are lying! I think you've got [the diamond] yourself!" Atherton says.

Atherton discovers the sleeping Mary and exerts his will on her. Hypnotized, Mary brings him the stone, and Atherton goes nearly crazy with joy as he fondles the diamond. He lunges lustfully at Mary. Wanda attacks her husband. John and Dakar run to help Mary but are attacked by Atherton's crew. Dakar prevails and rushes to rescue Mary. Wanda fatally stabs her husband. Atherton tries to atone by giving the diamond back to Mary, suggesting that she throw it into the ocean. John knocks out one of the last of Atherton's crew. Mary attempts to do Atherton's last bidding, but Dakar—finally acknowledged as a descendant of the priest in the 16th-century episodes—asks that the diamond be restored to its rightful place. John and Mary embrace in silhouette. A silhouette of Dakar, raising the diamond in one hand, follows this image.

And so *The Hope Diamond Mystery* comes to an end. Despite the soap-operatics, the overdone histrionics of most of the actors and the fact that director Stuart Paton is no D.W. Griffith, the serial is worth-while—especially for any admirer of Boris Karloff.

Paton was a well-respected director of silent films, but he never mastered the sound medium. He ended up making low-budget serials and melodramas in the 1930s for Hollywood's Poverty Row studios. While the camerawork is not as fluid as that of kindred European productions of the day—there is little camera mobility, for example—the photography is certainly comparable with what was being done in most American movies at the time. The subjective-vantage shots, looking from the caves and cliffs of the island at approaching characters, are fairly novel for a 1921 serial, and the dissolves of the statue seemingly appearing and disappearing are certainly inventive. The flashback sequences looked more expensively done than they could have been, lending weight to the script's implicit theme of reincarnation.

Boris Karloff's performance, however, lends the greatest interest today. Some 10 years before *Frankenstein*, Karloff gives a graceful, subtle performance, especially compared to the other actors. Karloff would play mysterious East Indian types over the long haul, from 1929's *The Unholy Night* to 1949's *Abbott and Costello Meet the Killer—Boris Karloff*, but never again would he play so sympathetic a Far Easterner as Dakar. Thanks to Scott Allen Nollen's detective work on Karloff's ancestry in *Boris Karloff: A Gentleman's Life*, we now know that Boris' grandmother on his father's side was East Indian. No doubt Karloff was taunted as a youngster about his darker skin. Perhaps Boris was coming to terms with his ancestry in this unexpected nuanced performance as the heroic Dakar. It is a superb characterization, particularly under the strenuous circumstances of serial production.

Toronto-born Grace Darmond (1898-1963), a major star only occasionally associated with serials, was in slight decline when she made *The Hope Diamond Mystery*, which she serves nicely but unspectacularly. Her career rallied and persisted on into 1927, but she retired with the advent of talking pictures. Harry Carter's villainy is hammy enough to call to mind the more over-ripe work of Bela Lugosi, as in *Shadow of Chinatown*. Carter's acting is still better than what one might expect from someone in this type of role—such as Paul Panzer in *The Perils of Pauline* (1914), wringing his hands in glee. George Chesebro is okay as

THE HOPE DIAMOND MYSTERY

The most sinister jewel in history

FEATURING -GRACE- DARMOND

A STUPENDOUS 15 EPISODE SERIAL

the hero. He wound up playing increasingly small roles in features and serials for many years to come.

Typical of the serial idiom, there are problems of story sense. James Marcon's shock-induced state of suspended animation is a bit much for audiences of any era to swallow. Elsewhere, one title card offers the preposterous revelation that Sidney Atherton has kept Mary under his hypnotic power for years. And wouldn't Nang Fu's Chinese gang members resent his patently Caucasian ethnicity? Despite all this silliness and the overriding soap opera subplotting, the serial bears rediscovery.

Some modern-day sources mention that some scenes were hand-tinted. The 16-millimeter archival copy screened for this book shows no color. A few scenes appear choppy, as if frames are missing from the 35mm nitrate source-print, but on the whole, the film plays agreeably well. Generally the lighting is vivid; a few very dark scenes suggest a black-and-white transfer from a tinted original.

The history of the Hope Diamond and its curse is as colorful as the serial itself. The jewel is a stunning blue, weighing in now at 44.52 carats, and takes its name from a former owner, Henry Philip Hope. It was mined in India, and legend holds that a thief took it from the eye of a holy statue. An adventurer named Tavernier (note the movie's subtle change in spelling) brought the then-112-carat diamond to France in 1668. The gem was sold to King Louis XIV, who had it cut into a 67-carat, heart-shaped stone and named it the Blue Diamond of the Crown. The story goes that Tavernier was killed by wild dogs on a return visit to India.

Louis XVI and Marie Antoinette inherited the diamond, which had become popularly known as the French Blue. Around the time of the

French Revolution in 1792, the diamond was stolen along with the other royal jewels. France never recovered it. A Goya painting, c. 1800, shows Queen Maria Louisa of Spain wearing a gem that looks remarkably like the French Blue. The diamond was at length tracked down and placed in safekeeping with a Dutch diamond cutter named Wilhelm Fals, who re-tooled it to its present size. Tragedy stalked the Fals family. By 1830, the diamond appeared in London and was bought by Henry Hope.

Later owners also were dogged by violent death, madness, political and economic ruin, and suicide. In 1947, New York jeweler Henry Winston bought a collection that included the Hope Diamond. Apparently nothing suggesting a curse happened to him, but at any rate he allowed the Smithsonian Institution to take it off his hands in 1958.

CREDITS: Producer: George Kleine; Director: Stuart Paton; Screen Adaptation: Charles Goddard and John B. Clymer; From the Life Story by: May Yohe, Formerly Lady Frances Hope; Photographed by: William Thornley; Personnel Supervision: L.C. Wheeler; British Title: *The Romance of the Hope Diamond*; a Serial in 15 Chapters; Released: February 19, 1921, by Kosmik Films; Copyrighted: 1920

CAST: Grace Darmond (Mary Hilton/Bibi); George Chesebro (John Gregge/Jean Baptiste Tavanier); Harry Carter (Sidney Atherton, aka Nang Fu/Ghung); William Marion (James Marcon/Bagi); Boris Karloff (Dakar/Priest of Kama-Sita); Carmen Phillips (Wanda Atherton/Mizra); William Buckley (Reginald Travers); May Yohe (Herself, the former Lady Frances Hope); Frank Seka (Saki); Harry Archer (Johnson); Captain Clayton (Lord Francis Hale); Ethel Shannon (Lady Frances Hale)

CHAPTER TITLES: 1) "The Hope Diamond Mystery"; 2) "The Vanishing Hand"; 3) "The Forged Note"; 4) "The Jewel of Sita"; 5) "A Virgin's Love" (in England, "The Mysterious Enemy"); 6) "The House of Terror"; 7) "The Flames of Despair"; 8) "Yellow Whisperings"; 9) "The Evil Eye"; 10) "In the Spider's Web"; 11) "The Cup of Fear"; 12) "The Ring of Death"; 13) "The Lash of Hate"; 14) "Primitive Passions"; 15) "An Island of Destiny"

THE RIDERS OF THE PLAINS
(Arrow Pictures; 1924)

His showy part in *The Hope Diamond Mystery* notwithstanding, Karloff found himself back among the small-role ranks in short order. Hedging his bets against a forced lapse from bit parts to crowd-extra work, Karloff retrenched into manual labor. His work with Eastman Builders Supply Co. involved the loading and cross-town trucking of heavy construction materials. The historian and filmmaker George E. Turner learned during the 1980s that Karloff's boss on this taxing job was "a guy named George Eastman—no kin to Kodak's George Eastman—who turned out to be the landlord at our Film Effects lab in Hollywood, where I worked from 1978 until about 1982 or '83. I'm convinced that the work ol' Boris did for this Eastman guy must have given him that bandy-legged aspect, not to mention the crippling problems with his back that he developed in his later years."

The Riders of the Plains, from independent Arrow Pictures, stars Jack Perrin, Marilyn Mills, Ruth Royce and Boris Karloff. Jack Perrin was a well-known matinee hero, destined for a less substantial career in the talking pictures. Miss Mills was exclusively identified with Westerns, with about a dozen shoot-'em-ups during the '20s including *Come On, Cowboys!* (1924), *The Rip Snorter* (1925) and *The Love of Paquita* (1927). Miss Royce's career spanned the same period, with a broader range of subject matter including *All Dolled Up* (1921) and *Caught Bluffing* (1922) before her own horse-opera typecasting kicked in with such titles as *Action Galore* (1925) and *Code of the Cow Country* (1927). Miss Royce specialized in impersonating villainous or fallen women.

Riders of the Plains was directed by Jacques Jaccard, an artist who stayed in the business for quite some time: Jaccard is credited as dialogue director in some of Universal's much later serials, including *Riders of Death Valley* and *Overland Mail* (1941-42). Serial scholar Jim Stringham has supplied a good idea of the plot. The significance and substance of Karloff's role remain unknown.

The yarn opens in St. Joseph, Missouri, on the eve of the Civil War in 1861. Johnnie Frey (Perrin), one of the "most fearless riders" of the Pony Express, is approaching the town when he spots a large encampment of

Indians. These chieftains are debating whether to wait for a treaty from Washington or declare war. Running Elk pleads for peace, while the younger Sitting Bull favors battle. Star Light (Miss Mills), Running Elk's daughter—who is actually a white girl, raised by the Indians since childhood—is among the gathering. Johnnie is spotted by Sitting Bull, but Star Light helps him escape. Frey learns that war has been declared between the North and the South. He tells the townspeople that the problem with the Indians needs settling first.

Landowner Jacques Cartier is trying to reclaim land lost under the Louisiana Purchase. He knows that Johnnie Frey—who has ties to the North—is interested in his daughter, as is Dan Morgan, whose sympathies lie with the South. Cartier tells his daughter Simone (Miss Royce) to keep both men interested in her. Cartier is an influential merchant, owning trading posts from New Orleans to Alaska. He sees the imminent treaty between Washington and the Indians as a threat to his regaining his land, so he tries to foil the peacemaking efforts.

Indian agents Bart Frey and Tom Kildare arrive to negotiate the treaty with the Indians. Just before the deadline, their stagecoach reaches the encampment, and it looks as though all is well. However, Dan Morgan and his raiders have been sent by Jacques Cartier. Morgan's gang starts a prairie fire. The Indians survive this and other attempts to balk the treaty.

Star Light and Johnnie fall in love. Running Elk decides it is time to tell his daughter that he is not her natural father. Sitting Bull provokes a division among the tribesmen. Cartier feels that an Indian uprising will be, in effect, a victory for the South. He plots to win back his land with the help of the Southern Rebels. Morgan gets the treaty away from the agents, but Star Light steals it back again. This hot-potato plot device is an old standby. Alfred Hitchcock was fond of using the same gimmick, which he called the Maguffin.

Dan Morgan redeems himself by saving Star Light's life before a full-scale war can break out between the Indians and the settlers. When the treaty is again delivered to the Indian agents and the tribes accept the agreement, Running Elk tells a defeated Cartier that Star Light is actually his daughter. During an earlier war, when Star Light was an infant, Cartier's wife died and the baby was accidentally abandoned. Cartier believed both his wife and daughter were killed, never knowing that Running Elk's tribe rescued the child. At this news, Cartier repents and all is forgiven. The father is reunited with his daughter. His other daughter, Simone, is now free to settle down with Dan Morgan. Johnnie Frey does likewise with Star Light.

It is probably a safe guess that Karloff had the role of an Indian or one of the raiders, parts he had played before. Already, he was becoming known as an actor suited to small villainous roles. Karloff had been working in movies for five tedious years now, and there must have been times when he wondered whether it was worth the trouble.

No contemporary reviews have turned up on this lost picture.

CREDITS: Director: Jacques Jaccard; Screenplay: Karl Coolidge and Jacques Jaccard; a Serial in 15 Chapters; Released: September 15, 1924

CAST: Jack Perrin (Johnnie Frey); Marilyn Mills (Star Light); Ruth Royce (Simone Cartier); and Charles Brinley, Kingsley Benedict, Running Elk [actor's name and character's name may be identical], Robert Miles, Rhody Hathaway, Clark Comstock, Boris Karloff; and Star, Beverly and Whiskey (horses)

CHAPTER TITLES: 1) "Red Shadows"; 2) "Dangerous Hazards"; 3) "A Living Death"; 4) "Flames of Fury"; 5) "Morgan's Raid"; 6) "Out of the Past"; 7) "A Fighting Gamble"; 8) "A Prisoner of War"; 9) "Pawns of Destiny"; 10) "Riding for Life"; 11) "In Death's Shadow"; 12) "Flaming Vengeance"; 13) "Thundering Hoofs"; 14) "Red Talons"; 15) "The Reckoning"

PERILS OF THE WILD
(Universal Pictures; 1925)

It was during this lean time, lasting over a year, that Karloff met and married his first wife, a dancer. Her name was Helene Vivian Soule, but her stage name was given variously as Polly and Pauline. In 1929, after Miss Soule left her husband to resettle in Panama, the couple filed for divorce. While employed as a truck driver, Karloff would be able to take a day or two off if a film role came his way. By 1925, he was working again—not much, perhaps, but working all the same—as an actor.

Perils of the Wild stars Joe Bonomo, along with Margaret Quimby, Jack Mower and other actors. Modern-day researchers generally agree that Karloff also graces the cast. Joe Bonomo was one of the top stuntmen

AN ADVENTURE PICTURE

"PERILS of the WILD"

BASED ON THE THRILLING "The SWISS FAMILY ROBINSON" ADVENTURES OF

FEATURING JOE BONOMO

AND MARGARET QUIMBY

DIRECTED BY FRANCIS FORD

CHAPTER 3 - THE FLAMING JUNGLE

of the silent era, handily in a league with the great Yakima Canutt—at least during Bonomo's heyday of the 1920s. Solidly built, Bonomo was a ruggedly handsome man.

Perils' director is Francis Ford. Francis, John Ford's older brother, was well known as a director in the silent-screen days. It is ironic that as he started to slip in popularity as a director, his brother started his climb to recognition as one of the screen's finer directors. (It's interesting that Boris Karloff thought himself well directed as the religious fanatic in John Ford's 1934 picture *The Lost Patrol*; many fans feel that Ford had Karloff *over*acting.) By the time sound movies became established, Francis Ford found that his silent-era style was out of fashion and he became a character actor instead. A good example is Francis' mysterious hermit in the Buck Jones serial, *Gordon of Ghost City* (1933). Out of family loyalty, and despite a lengthy, personally resentful estrangement with his brother, Francis Ford continued to appear in many of John Ford's films, usually in small but showy roles.

Only fundamental plot information has turned up. Historian Bill G. "Buck" Rainey crystallizes it like so: After a fight in a pub in Liverpool while in the process of getting a crew together, the Swiss family Robinson set sail for Australia with a cargo of flint-locks and gunpowder and, unknowingly, with a pirate crew. Another passenger, Emily Montrose, proves to be the heroine. The ship is seized by the crew. A storm follows, and the pirates abandon the ship and row to a tropical island, their headquarters. The Robinsons land on the other side of the island, believing it

Perils of the Wild: **Joe Bonomo and Margaret Quimby**

uninhabited except for the well-mannered animals. They prepare to adjust themselves to their new home. "The adventures that follow are many," adds Rainey in a tantalizing coda.

Obviously, the yarn derives from Johann David Wyss' classic novel of 1899, *Swiss Family Robinson*, which would receive a more formally official adaptation in an RKO-Radio feature of 1940. The book certainly has the right ingredients for a serial, right down to the episodic structure. *Perils'* screenplay was handled by Isadore Bernstein and William Lord Wright. Wyss, a Swiss pastor, obviously was inspired by Daniel Defoe's *Robinson Crusoe* in creating a tale that he first related in spoken form to his four sons. Later, one son, Johann Rudolph Wyss, convinced the storyteller that the tale had possibilities as a novel. Several filmed versions followed, including a popularly beloved Disney feature of 1960, the teleseries *Lost in Space* (originally conceived as *Space Family Robinson*) and its much later feature-film spin-off, and a strikingly true-to-Wyss telefeature in 1975. *Perils of the Wild* is the one *Robinson* adaptation that must be considered lost.

Historian Jim Stringham has turned up a *Perils* still that shows an actor who looks quite a bit like Boris Karloff. This image appeared in Joe Bonomo's autobiography, *The Strong Man*.

Perils of the Wild: **One face in this crowd bears a strong resemblance to Karloff.**

By the time Karloff made his next serial, *Vultures of the Sea*, he had spent more than 10 years in Hollywood. Karloff was known, if not by any vast filmgoing public, at least by the film industry as a reliable character actor with a gift for villainy—or "heavy men," as the specialty was termed in the movie business' casting directories. Stardom was still a distant prospect.

CREDITS: Director: Francis Ford; Screenplay: Isadore Bernstein and William Lord Wright; Based upon *Swiss Family Robinson* by Johann David Wyss; a Serial in 15 Chapters; Released: August 27, 1925

CAST: Joe Bonomo (Frederick Robinson); Margaret Quimby (Emily Montrose); Jack Mower (Sir Charles Liecester); Alfred Allen (Captain William Robinson); Eva Gordon (Frau Mitilla Robinson); Jack Murphy (Jack Robinson); Howard Enstedt (Ernest Robinson); Francis Erwin (Francis Robinson); William Dyer (Black John); Albert Prisco (Tonie); Fannie Warren (Bonita); John Wallace (Pirate); James Welsh (Pirate); Phil Ford (Pirate); Sammy Gervon (Pirate) and [presumably] Boris Karloff (Pirate)

CHAPTER TITLES: 1) "The Hurricane"; 2) "The Lion's Fangs"; 3) "The Flaming Jungle"; 4) "The Treasure Cave"; 5) "Saved By the Sun"; 6) "The Jungle Trail"; 7) "Pirate Peril"; 8) "Winds of Fate"; 9) "Rock of Revenge"; 10) "The Rescue"; 11) "The Stolen Wedding"; 12) "Marooned"; 13) "Prisoners of the Sea"; 14) "The Leopard's Lair"; 15) "In the Nick of Time"

VULTURES OF THE SEA
(Mascot Pictures Corp.; 1928)

Mascot Pictures was a little independent studio that was just as scrappy and energetic as its boss, Nat Levine. The pudgy, bespectacled thrill-merchant ran his studio with a steady hand and a tight fist, but he worked hard and expected likewise of his employees and stars. Their dedication to craft still shows on the screen—an artistry that is more raw energy than polished accomplishment, but generously entertaining all the same.

It is important to remember that in the late 1920s, Mascot Pictures was not all that different, in attitude or in physical properties, from rival Harry Cohn's Columbia Pictures. Not even MGM, Paramount, Warner Bros. or Universal had yet developed the glamour and vastness for which such names are known today. Nat Levine's independently produced serials posed stiff competition for both the majors and the minors.

Vultures of the Sea was well received by its intended audience and by some of the press as well. The serial format had not yet fallen completely into the category of children's entertainment.

The story concerns the bad reputation of a sailing ship, the *Scorpion*. Its owner, Captain Enright (Joseph Mack) is murdered. Armstrong (J.P. Lockney), an innocent man, is convicted. His son Frank (Johnnie Walker) sets out to prove Armstrong's innocence by going aboard on the next voyage to find the guilty party. He meets Ruth Enright (Shirley Mason), daughter of the murdered owner, and they fall in love. The brutal Captain Hawley (Tom Santschi) complicates matters. There is another murder, of which Frank is accused. Ruth is cast adrift. Eventually, the young couple survives to discover the murderer—and to claim a sunken treasure.

Boris Karloff's character is called Grouchy, a name that seems to fit his appearance in one surviving still. Among the screenwriters is Wyndham "Windy" Gittens, a familiar name to the serial buff. Gittens also had been a film editor, and he tried his hand at directing—only once, filling in for B. Reeves "Breezy" Eason one day during the making of the 1932 serial *The Last of the Mohicans* (1932).

In its review of *Vultures*, the show-biz publication *Bioscope* cited "a constant succession of desperate conflicts, knife-throwing, mutinies and

An atmospheric shot of the nasty-looking crew from *Vultures of the Sea*, with an eminently recognizable Boris Karloff.

hairbreadth escapes," adding that "as the characters are justly termed 'the scum of the seas,' the events do not appear unlikely. There is a fine crowd of well-differentiated ruffians."

When Boris Karloff was hired to play one of the cutthroats, he was starting to garner attention in Hollywood, but only as a dependable character actor. In a sense, Karloff was already typecast, and had not a stage play called *The Criminal Code* come along in 1929—affording him another hoodlum role, but one of lead-challenging intensity—Karloff might have remained mired in the sub-supporting ranks.

Karloff was an extremely talented actor, but no doubt also an extremely lucky one. While clearly typecast for the long term of stardom, he took the typecasting to one plateau after another, moving beyond the limited perceptions of his early-day employers. When interviewed some 30 years later by radio announcer Colin Edwards, Karloff spoke with the philosophical wisdom of advanced age and vast experience.

In a surviving tape recording, Edwards asks Karloff about typecasting: "[Y]ou haven't resented it, then?" Karloff replies: "Good heavens, no! I mean if, after all, an actor is in business. He's there to sell his services, isn't he? ...I think that if an actor gets a trademark handed to him on a silver platter, he's a jolly lucky man!"

Bela Lugosi in 1928 was already a star on Broadway, with his mesmerizing role in *Dracula*. Lugosi was as confident in his future as Karloff was uncertain in his.

No print of *Vultures of the Sea* is known to have survived.

CREDITS: Producer: Nat Levine. Director: Richard Thorpe; Story: Wyndham Gittens and William Burt; a Serial in 10 Chapters; Released: August 1, 1928

CAST: Shirley Mason (Ruth Enright); Johnnie Walker (Frank Armstrong); Tom Santschi (Captain Hawley); Arthur Dewey (Limpy); Boris Karloff (Grouchy); Frank Hagney (Mate); John Carpenter (Cook); Joseph Mack (Captain Enright); George Magrill (Sea Lawyer); J.P. Lockney (Mr. Armstrong); Joe Bennett (Dummy); Lafe McKee (Frenchy)

CHAPTER TITLES: 1) "The Hell Ship"; 2) "Cast Adrift"; 3) "Driven to Port"; 4) "Scum of the Seas"; 5) "Harbor of Danger" (given elsewhere as "The Harbor of Danger"); 6) "The Stolen Ship"; 7) "At the Mercy of the Flames"; 8) "The Fight for Possession"; 9) "The Traitor"; 10) "The End of the Quest"

THE VANISHING RIDER
(Universal Pictures Corp.; 1928)

True to its name, *The Vanishing Rider* has vanished—yet another lost film.

To begin at the beginning—**Chapter No. 1: "The Road Agent"**—we can resort to materials discovered by Jim Stringham. The formal plot synopsis was drafted for copyright-protection purposes. Butch Bradley (Bud Osborne), owner of the Golden Chance Saloon, is also the boss of an outlaw gang. Most of his crooked activities are blamed on the mysterious Vanishing Rider. Bradley, eager to exploit a gold strike on the nearby Allen ranch, hatches a scheme to drive the owner, Mary Allen (Ethlyne

CHAPTER I
THE ROAD AGENT

A lobby card from *The Vanishing Rider*, a long-misplaced Western serial whose cast includes Boris Karloff.

Clair), away. Bradley's last robbery fared none too well: The Vanishing Rider stole the loot right out from under the gang.

Secret Service Agent Jim Davis (William Desmond) poses as foreman of the Allen Ranch and visits the saloon to check up on Bradley. A campaign is launched to capture the Vanishing Rider. The Rider, meanwhile, hides out at the ranch. Mary finds herself fascinated by the mysterious stranger and helps him escape. Butch accelerates his plans for the Allen ranch, starting a stampede and placing Mary in mortal danger.

Chapter No. 2: "Trapped" finds the Rider rescuing Mary. He returns to her the gold from the earlier robbery, but will answer no questions. Bradley sees the Vanishing Rider from a distance. Jim Davis and

Mary's uncle, "Pop" Smith (Nelson McDowell), learn from Mary what has happened. Butch tricks Mary into heading for town, so that he can kidnap her for a ransom he is certain the Vanishing Rider will pay. Mary's uncle gets a posse together quickly, but the gang is ready for them.

The Rider demands that the crooks free Mary, for he has brought a ransom. The gang captures the Rider, locks Mary in another room and then escapes. The posse arrives. The sheriff gets a shock when he unmasks the Vanishing Rider.

Chapter No. 3: "A Fight for Life" starts out as the sheriff discovers that the mystery man is Jim Davis. Despite Davis' law-enforcement credentials, the sheriff arrests him. Meanwhile, the gang learns that the loot is worthless. The sheriff takes Davis into town, where he sees the Vanishing Rider. He releases Davis and sets out in pursuit. The Rider escapes. Jim and Mary take the gold to the sheriff's office for safekeeping.

Jim walks into a trap while trailing a gangster. The Vanishing Rider joins Jim in a brawl. The Rider shoots out the lights.

Chapter No. 4: "Brother Against Brother" The synopsis, neglecting to finesse the cliffhanger at the end of the prior chapter, resumes the tale with Butch Bradley's decision that he has waited too long to take over the Allen ranch. While Mary meets up with the Vanishing Rider at the ranch, she tells him that Jim Davis has sworn that he'd capture the masked hombre. The Vanishing Rider laughs off the threat, but Mary pleads with him to give up the outlaw life. At that moment, Jim Davis holds the Vanishing Rider at gunpoint. Mary forces Jim to let the outlaw escape, reminding Jim about the time the Rider had saved him.

The gang attacks the ranch. Mary is kidnapped, and a fire starts in the barn, trapping Jim. The Rider heads toward the barn as the rafters collapse.

Chapter No. 5: "The Wings of Fury" begins with the fire. Mary falls into a well. Jim, searching for her, lands in the well. The Rider saves them, finds a will left by Mary's father and gives the will to Bradley. Bradley forges an advantageous version of the will, but the Rider secretly takes the original will.

Jim and Mary discover that the barn had hidden an entrance to the mine. Bradley shows up with the forged will. Bradley decides now is as good time as any to take over, but first he turns in for the night. The Rider sneaks in and discovers the forged will. He finds himself held at gunpoint by Jim. As the Rider is about to explain, Bradley breaks in and opens fire.

Chapter No. 6: "The False Message" reveals that Butch's gunfire has struck no one. The Rider has hightailed it with the forged will, and now there is no evidence that Bradley owns the ranch. Bradley has no choice but to leave. Mary, refusing to believe that the Vanishing Rider would steal the will, intends to make some kind of settlement with Bradley. She is not convinced that the will she saw was a forgery. Bradley sends Mary a fake message, inviting her to meet the Rider. Bradley secretly follows her. The Rider tells Mary to return the will to Jim.

The gang follows Mary. The Rider opens fire, driving the mob away. Jim sets out after Mary and sees her astride the Rider's horse. Jim inadvertently causes the Rider and Mary to go tumbling down a cliff.

Chapter No. 7: "The Waters of Death" finds the Rider and Mary safe. Mary takes possession of the real will and learns of Bradley's treacheries. Mary decides to hide the will within the entrance to the mine. A Bradley henchman, spying on her, lets the boss know he has discovered the entryway. The gang surrounds the ranchers, and a stray bullet cracks a floodgate latch, releasing a deluge.

Chapter No. 8: "The Bargain of Fear" begins as the Rider swims to the floodgates and manages to close them. Jim insists that Mary tell him the location of the Rider's hideout. She rides away to warn the Rider; Jim follows. The Rider informs Bradley he will strike a bargain.

The Rider plans to dynamite the entrance to his cave and capture the gang. Bradley and his gang show up, and the Rider demands a written agreement. He looks up to see Jim and Mary standing at the entrance. He runs toward them, hoping to save them from the explosion, which comes a moment too soon.

Chapter No. 9: "The Last Stand" opens as the Rider blocks his friends from the explosion, taking the brunt of the blast. When he regains consciousness, Jim is holding him at gunpoint. The mysterious document makes it look as though the Rider is in cahoots with Bradley, and Jim takes him to the ranch to meet the sheriff. Jim's summons to the law is overheard by a henchman.

Bradley demands that Jim hand over the Vanishing Rider to him, which Jim reluctantly does. Bradley discovers that the Rider has destroyed the incriminating agreement. Bradley's gang overtakes Mary's car, which crashes over an embankment.

Chapter No. 10: "Vengeance" opens with the crash of the car carrying Mary and Jim. The Rider shows up in time to rescue them. He also takes the incriminating agreement from Jim. Later, Jim tells the sheriff all he knows. Bradley and his gang make a strategic exit, but the Rider stops their stagecoach.

The Sheriff takes the gang and the Vanishing Rider to jail, where Jim finally explains that he and the Rider are brothers. They have been working secretly to capture Bradley. Mary's dilemma has not been resolved: Which of the brothers will she choose? Thus ends the copyright synopsis.

One may surmise that Boris Karloff plays one of the henchmen. Karloff, at this point, would likely be a prominent member of the gang, much as Lon Chaney, Jr. would play similar parts on the way up. No documentation has come to light, apart from a distinct likelihood of Karloff's presence, agreed upon by a number of credentialed researchers.

The Vanishing Rider would be Karloff's only serial for Universal Pictures. The director, Ray Taylor (1888-1952), was one of Universal's top serial directors. Taylor began his career as a stage actor and manager. After serving in World War I, he landed in Hollywood and was employed as an assistant director at Fox Film Corp., working with the up-and-coming John Ford. As late as the 1933 Universal chapter play *Gordon of Ghost City*, Taylor was still doing first-rate work. Taylor co-directed serials (often with Ford Beebe) at Universal into the early 1940s. A drinking problem seems to have rendered his later work erratic.

In 1971, Buster Crabbe told George E. Turner and Michael H. Price that Ray Taylor's unacknowledged direction of *Flash Gordon* (1936) was "the stuff that really held that picture together." However, Taylor's handling of *The Return of Chandu* (1934), starring Bela Lugosi, shows a decline in pace and dramatic tension. Later along, Taylor made a particularly impressive feature, *The Michigan Kid* (1947), with Jon Hall, Victor McLaglen, Rita Johnson and Andy Devine, but Taylor more often stuck with low-budget Westerns such as *Mark of the Lash* and *Son of Billy the Kid* (1948-49).

The Vanishing Rider derives from an original story by William Lord Wright, one of Universal's top writers, who doubled as an executive in the serial department. Rock-jawed leading man William Desmond was born in Dublin in 1878 but was raised in New York. Desmond began making films in 1915, trading upon a strong reputation from Vaudeville and the legitimate stage, and rapidly became a significant star of action pictures and serials.

Desmond turned 50 in 1928, a pivotal year in the transition from silent pictures to talkies. He retrenched as a secondary player in the talking pictures, finally retiring in 1940. Desmond was married to Mary McIvor, who occasionally worked as an actress. Eventually his granddaughter, Mary Jo Desmond, would play the adopted daughter of Lon Chaney, Jr. in *The Last Frontier* in 1932. William Desmond himself landed a small role in that serial. He died in 1949, not long after his 70th birthday.

The Vanishing Rider's spunky leading lady, Ethlyne Clair, has been described by historian Kalton Lahue as "a happy extrovert who loved people and social standing." Adds Lahue: "She had the drive and ambition..., [but it was] her misfortune to arrive just as silent film was being dealt its death blow."

CREDITS: Director: Ray Taylor; Screenplay: George H. Plympton; Story: William Lord Wright; Photographed by: Val Cleveland; a Serial in 10 Chapters; Released: January 16, 1928

CAST: William Desmond (Jim Davis); Ethlyne Clair (Mary Allen); Nelson McDowell (Pop Smith); Bud Osborne [given elsewhere as Osbourne]; Butch Bradley; and [presumably] Boris Karloff

CHAPTER TITLES: 1) "The Road Agent"; 2) "Trapped"; 3) "A Fight For Life"; 4)"Brother Against Brother"; 5) "The Wings of Fury"; 6) "The False Message"; 7) "The Waters of Death"; 8) "The Bargain of Fear"; 9) "The Last Stand"; 10) "Vengeance"

THE FATAL WARNING
(Mascot Pictures Corp.; 1929)

The Fatal Warning (1929) is the last of the silent serials known or believed to feature Boris Karloff—and the last of the lost ones. A press book, supplied by researcher Jim Stringham, contains pitches and exploitation tips designed to lure children to the box-office. Only a few years beforehand, the serial makers were still targeting a broader family

Karloff's character is at the wrong end of a knife in *The Fatal Warning*.

audience. One suggestion—which has long since become a standard practice—was to offer a special matinee at reduced prices. A more extravagant suggestion:

> Perhaps you can tie up with your local
> schools to have the school children in their
> English study classes write short stories
> around the title of The Fatal Warning and
> then award the winning story... some sub-
> stantial prize. The prize should be some
> small money prize... in addition to tickets
> in the theater... Every child will be full of
> the idea and will immediately work on it

at home, enlisting the aid of the parents. The prize should not be given out until the last chapter of the serial is played. In the meantime, you will not only get regular publicity all through the run of the picture, but also many of these children will come with their parents regularly to get ideas for the story, which is natural.

Lacking a chapter-by-chapter synopsis, one is tempted to follow the lead of that exploitation tip. But no, a more reliable synopsis exists in simplified form: Banker William Rogers (George Periolat) is reading a mystery novel, *The Fatal Warning*, one night when confronted by a mysterious intruder and—apparently—killed. Whatever his fate, Rogers is held responsible for the theft of $100,000. His daughter, Dorothy Rogers (Helene Costello), knowing that her father had enemies, sets out to prove his innocence and hires a private investigator, Russell Thorne (Ralph Graves). The only clue is a footprint, which reveals a scar.

Suspects are numerous: bank president John Harmon (Tom Lingham); a butler who mysteriously resigns and a fake butler who takes his place; golf course manager Norman Brooks (Lloyd Whitlock); Marie Jordan (Symona Boniface); Leonard Taylor (Phillips Smalley); and Smoky Joe, a friend of William Rogers. Also among the characters are a mysterious aviator and a bearded man, in those days when a beard betokened either distinction or menace.

Dorothy and Russell find themselves threatened by gunfire and abducted. Along the way, they fall in love and solve the mystery. William Rogers is discovered alive and well, manipulating the investigation from the sidelines.

Ralph Graves and Helene Costello were popular stars at the time, with numerous feature-film credits sprinkled throughout the decade. Fans of the Three Stooges will take particular note of an early-in-the-game appearance by Symona Boniface, whose feature-film career did not pick up steam until the early 1930s. Miss Boniface is best remembered today as a high-society matron in collision with the Stooges, serving the team much as Margaret Dumont would serve as a foil for Groucho Marx. Boris Karloff plays a character called Mullins, an employee at the bank. The tradepaper *Kinematograph Weekly* published this opinion: "The story is sufficiently interesting to make one look forward to the next episode; consequently the usual absurd culminating thrill does not figure at the end of each episode, while the characters are interpreted by a capable cast."

The English film scholar Denis Gifford reveals that the U.K. release was given new titles for its individual chapters, in addition to a re-editing job to subdue the melodramatic elements in order to appeal to more sophisticated audiences.

CREDITS: Producer: Nat Levine; Director: Richard Thorpe; Story: Wyndham Gittens; Production Supervisor: Ben Schwab; a Serial in 10 Chapters; Released: February 15, 1929

CAST: Helene Costello (Dorothy Rogers); Ralph Graves (Russell Thorne); Tom Lingham (John Harman); Phillips Smalley (Leonard Taylor); Lloyd Whitlock (Norman Brooks); George Periolat (William Rogers); Boris Karloff (Mullins); Syd Crossley (Dawson); Martha Mattox (Mrs. Charles Peterson); Symona Boniface (Marie Jordan)

CHAPTER TITLES: 1) "A Midnight Mystery" [in England: "An Intruder at Midnight," aka "Enter Russell Thorne"]; 2) "The Phantom Flyer" [in England: "The Enemy Shows His Hand"]; 3) "The Crash of Doom" [in England: "Rescue by Plane"]; 4) "The Pit of Peril" [in England: "The Message on the Wall"]; 5) "The Clutching Hand" [in England: "Suspects All"]; 6) "Into Thin Air" [in England: "The Clue of the Footprints]; 7) "The House of Horror" [in England: "The Blank Sheet"]; 8) "The Fatal Fumes" [in England: "The Banker's Promise,"]; 9) "By Whose Hand?" [in England: "Traitor at the Trial"]; 10) "Unmasked" [in England: "Taylor Unmasked"]

KING OF THE KONGO
(Mascot Pictures Corp.; 1929)

Ford Beebe, Jr., son of the great serial director, told me of the times he would listen to his father and fellow director Joe Kane, "sitting around the dining-room table at home, arguing whether talking pictures would ever completely take silent films out of the business, and I can hear my Dad right now saying that he could see where talking pictures had some appeal, but he thought that—at that time, anyway—there was a certain effect of [printed] titles that would be lost with trying to say it! I think that was typical of other places around the business at that time."

The industry's dogged faith in the persistence of silent movies notwithstanding, Mascot honcho Nat Levine was loading his production budgets squarely in the favor of the newfangled talkies: Levine gave *Warning* short shrift in the name-brand casting department in order to afford the expensive sound-recording technology that he intended to try out on *Kongo*.

King of the Kongo seems no longer to exist in its authentic form. It was released as both a silent and as a part-talking serial. As such, it is credited as the first sound serial. Prints of the silent version have apparently disappeared, but prints of the sound version have turned up, minus the soundtrack. The audio was recorded on heavy shellac discs by the Victor Talking Machine Co. of Camden, N.J., using the Vitaphone system that had been established as an industry standard by Warner Bros.' well-received part-talker, *The Jazz Singer* (1927). While Fox Film Corp. was using the more efficient sound-on-film process called Movietone,

A mysterious looking Boris Karloff from *King of the Kongo*.

Macklin (Karloff) and a henchman plot evil deeds in *King of the Kongo*.

many studios stuck with the Vitaphone system. Only in recent years have significant numbers of other films' soundtrack disks turned up. Recently Ron Hutchinson of the film restoration organization The Vitaphone Project related that a collector in Michigan had a few of the long-lost Victor soundtrack disks from *King of the Kongo*. The collector (John Johnson) had disks for Chapters 4, 5, 7, 8 and 10. Mr. Johnson explained the disks are 16 inches in diameter. Like old radio transcription disks, they were recorded at the speed of 33 and 1/3, and the playback needle starts at the inside groove near the turntable spindle rather than the outside groove. Sound technicians discovered the fidelity of the recordings decreased as the size of the grooves increased. Several of the disks are slightly cracked; however, modern technology may soon be able to solve that problem and fans can hear this first talking serial.

As the film stands now, there are sequences where narrative and dialogue cards were inserted, but there are also sequences where full sound must have been used. In the first chapter, for instance, a Secret Service official (Richard Tucker) makes a speech about the dangers that Larry Trent (Walter Miller) will face in the African Congo when he goes after a gang of ivory thieves and, not incidentally, in search of his missing brother. While it is not impossible to figure out what is going on during the now-silenced all-dialogue portions, neither is it easy.

The sets showing the ruins of a temple are highly atmospheric, with many secret passageways and ominous shadows. There are striking images of wild animals and atmospheric shots of the suspected villain, Boris Karloff.

Larry Trent assembles a safari. Natives warn him to stay away from a dilapidated temple, where there lurks a gorilla known as the King of the Kongo. The fearsome-looking gorilla is played by one of the movies' greatest stuntmen, Joe Bonomo—star player of 1925's *Perils of the Wild*.

Larry explores the ruins and finds traces of a treasure. At a trading post, he meets Diana Martin (Jacqueline Logan), beautiful ward of a local missionary. Diana shows Larry a fragment of treasure that matches one he had found. Diana is looking for her long-vanished father, who had given her the artifact. Larry believes the disappearance of his brother and the disappearance of the girl's father may be connected. The ruins would be a likely place for a gangsters' hideout.

The crooks are apparently led by Scarface Macklin (Karloff), who has temporarily lost his memory—for it turns out that he is actually Diana's father. Larry and Diana face the gorilla, the gangsters and other perils. Finally, Diana's father regains his wits—only to die moments afterward. Larry finds his missing brother, and Diana and Larry find the lost treasure.

Karloff acted in *King of the Kongo* for a salary of $75 a week. The serial was shot in three weeks. Jacqueline Logan, a former Ziegfield Follies chorine, had recently won fame for her role as Mary Magdalene in Cecil B. DeMille's *The King of Kings* (1927). Heroic Walter Miller was a veteran of the serials. Richard Neill, seen as a prisoner, later would overplay the villain in Lon Chaney, Jr.'s first serial, *The Last Frontier* (1932). Director Richard Thorpe was a former Vaudeville comedian who finally landed in the big time at MGM in the middle 1930s.

Nat Levine spent $40,000 to produce this serial—almost an epic-scale budget for an independent production. A $5,000 line item went to the disk recordings, which Levine personally delivered across the continent to the Victor company for processing and duplication.

Lee Zahler's musical score includes the unusual touch of a romantic ballad, "Love Thoughts of You," which also was used as a dramatic

For a few brief moments father and daughter are reunited in *King of the Kongo*.

leitmotif. The composer's later work includes a haunting theme for *The Whispering Shadow* (1933) and a weird, frenzied score for *The Lost City* (1935). He later scored many of Columbia's serials. Zahler's son, Gordon Zahler, also went into the business of film scoring; Gordon is best known as arranger of the music for Edward D. Wood, Jr.'s *Plan 9 from Outer Space* (1959).

The trade publication *Bioscope* reviewed *King of the Kongo* in generically vague terms: "[It] retains everything that admirers of these melodramatic serials love to contemplate. Jacqueline Logan and Walter Miller impersonate the leading characters, and many well-known players give good support."

Although the surviving footage packs its own fascination, we hardly can develop much in the way of opinions on *King of the Kongo* unless its soundtrack platters turn up. The LS Video label has offered a videocassette edition of the surviving footage.

CREDITS: Producer: Nat Levine. Director: Richard Thorpe; Music: Lee Zahler; a Serial in 10 Chapters; Silent Version: 18,760 feet; Sound Version: 212 minutes; Released: August 20, 1929

CAST: Jacqueline Logan (Diana Martin); Walter Miller (Larry Trent); Richard Tucker (Secret Service Chief); Boris Karloff (Macklin); Larry Steers (Jack Drake); Harry Todd (Commodore); Richard Neil (Prisoner); Lafe McKee (Trader John); J.P. Lockney [given elsewhere as Leckrey] (Priest); William Burt (Mooney); Gordon Russell (Derelict); Robert Frazer [given on-screen as Frazier] (Native); Ruth Davis (Poppy); Joe Bonomo (Gorilla)

CHAPTER TITLES: 1) "Into the Unknown"; 2) "Terrors of the Jungle"; 3) "The Temple of the Beasts"; 4) "Gorilla Warfare"; 5) "Danger in the Dock"; 6) "The Fight at the Lion's Pit"; 7) "The Fatal Moment"; 8) Sentenced to Death"; 9) "Desperate Chances"; 10) "Jungle Justice"

KING OF THE WILD
(Mascot Pictures Corp.; 1931)

In hopes of proving himself innocent of the murder of an East Indian Rajah, adventurer Robert Grant (Walter Miller) is told to visit the seedy Inn of the Fez, which is run by a shady character called Mustapha. Boris Karloff gleefully plays Mustapha in his next-to-last serial assignment. Grant asks Mustapha to help him track down a man who had helped to frame him. That very man, known as Harris (Tom Santschi), approaches Mustapha. Mustapha cleverly states that the disguised Grant is looking for work. Harris, an animal trainer and treasure hunter, tells Grant that he can always use another worker.

Grant leaves as Mustapha and Harris discuss their own business, the raiding of a diamond mine found by a young explorer named Tom Armitage (Carroll Nye). Armitage has accidentally revealed his discovery, mistaking Harris for a diamond merchant. Mustapha plans to use the alluring Mrs. LaSalle (Dorothy Christie) to coax the secret from the youngster.

Karloff's shifty eyes and furtive moves are a joy to watch. His broad French-Arabian accent is also a treat—and reminiscent, too, of Bela Lugosi's occasional Asian impersonations.

Grant stows away when he discovers that Harris and his cargo of wild animals—including an apelike man named Bimi (Cyril McLaglen)— are taking an ocean trip. A Secret Service agent named Peterson (Victor Potel) is also under suspicion. Mrs. LaSalle is murdered. The ship is

Nat Levine presents

KING of the WILD

an ALL-TALKING SERIAL
IN TWELVE STIRRING CHAPTERS

with WALTER MILLER · NORA LANE · DOROTHY CHRISTY · TOM SANTSCHI
BORIS KARLOFF · VICTOR POTEL and ARTHUR McLAGLEN

Directed by RICHARD THORPE

A MASCOT SERIAL

CHAPTER 6 "The Creeping Doom"

wrecked by a typhoon, and the animals escape. The survivors who reach shore include Grant, Muriel Armitage (Nora Lane) and her brother Tom, as well as Harris, Mustapha and Bimi.

Tom Armitage is kidnapped and taken to a hideout in the desert. Tom refuses to tell where the diamond strike is located. Mustapha decides to lower Tom into a tiger pit, but Tom is able to escape. Complicating the proceedings are a Secret Service man disguised as an old woman and a mysterious man wearing black glasses.

Grant discovers the mine in the crater of the volcano. He finds himself under attack by Mustapha. Government troops capture Mustapha and his henchmen. Harris tries to escape but is thrown over a cliff in a horseback accident. Bimi carries his master away to a final resting place. Grant, now cleared, is free to find happiness with Muriel Armitage.

To present-day viewers, *King of the Wild* may seem crude and monotonous. On the plus side, the serial poses an engaging exercise in keeping track of the many outlandish developments. Karloff has nothing particularly well written with which to work, but he conveys admirably the treachery of the character.

Technically, the serial is quite an achievement for a little studio like Mascot. Ford Beebe, Jr. explained some of the problems in shooting such a production, for he worked on a similar outdoor serial the following year, *The Last of the Mohicans*.

The heroic Robert Grant faces peril at the hands of Mustapha in *King of the Wild*.

The cast and crew, Beebe explained:

> Worked so long that the sun would go
> down, and in order to make their sched-
> ule, they would have to shoot close-ups
> and things after dark, and light them arti-
> ficially. Well, they carried battery packs—
> just dry-cell battery packs—and incandes-
> cent lights, and the lights just weren't
> bright enough. So they tended to use...
> magnesium flares, and that gave them a
> nice, bright light, but they made so much
> noise that they couldn't [record] the sound.
> So we'd be standing around there after
> dark holding these flares.
>
> [M]ost of those outdoor serials were
> made in the summertime... so you could
> work 14 to 16 hours [a day]. We shot 'til it
> got so dark that you couldn't make out a

Mustapha is captured in this lobby card scene from *King of the Wild*.

> medium shot, even, and then they'd shoot
> close-ups against a tree...

For modern audiences—especially talking-picture serial fans who have grown accustomed to wall-to-wall music—the absence of any music (apart from the main titles) takes some getting used to. The so-called silent films of cinema's first few decades were in fact anything but silent, for although they lacked soundtracks they were meant to be accompanied by music, whether from a solo organ or a symphony orchestra. Audiences attending early talking films were disoriented when hearing musical scores underlining the dialogue and sound effects. Historian George E. Turner has explained that "musical backgrounds were considered an artifact of the silent film and unreal in the talkies."

Producer Hal Roach, partly in response to the insistence of English-born music-hall veteran Stan Laurel, helped to pioneer the scoring of talking pictures—both for dramatic effect and to obscure the hiss of the early-day sound-recording technology. In 1932, with Max Steiner's

Robert Grant is captured by Mustapha and his gang in *King of the Wild*.

groundbreaking score for *Symphony of Six Million* at RKO-Radio Pictures, musically scored films became popular once again. Even so, a number of low-budget producers, including Nat Levine, continued to release their films with music chiefly for the main titles and end titles.

CREDITS: Producer: Nat Levine; Director: Richard Thorpe; Screenplay and Story: Wyndham Gittens and Ford Beebe; Photographed by: Benjamin Kline and Edward Kull; Musical Direction: Lee Zahler; Assistant Directors: Theodore Joos and Lionel Backus; Sound Recording: George Lowerre, Disney Sound Recording Co.; a Serial in 12 Chapters, 248 minutes; Released: March 1, 1931

CAST: Walter Miller (Robert Grant); Nora Lane (Muriel Armitage); Dorothy Christy (Mrs. LaSalle); Tom Santschi (Harris); Boris Karloff (Mustapha); Cyril McLaglen (Bimi); Carroll Nye (Tom Armitage); Victor Potel (Peterson); Martha Lalande (Mrs. Colby); Mischa Auer (Dakka); Lafe McKee (Officer); and Otto Hoffman, Fletcher Norton, Albert De Winton [given elsewhere as De Warton], Merrill McCormick, Earle Douglas, Larry Steers, Eileen Schofield, Walter Ferdna, Norman Fenster [given elsewhere as Feusier], Dick LaReno, Floyd Shakelford

CHAPTER TITLES: 1) "The Tiger of Destiny"; 2) "Man Eaters"; 3) "The Avenging Horde"; 4) "The Secret of the Volcano"; 5) "The Pit of Peril"; 6) "The Creeping Doom"; 7) "Sealed Lips"; 8) "The Jaws of the Jungle"; 9) "The Door of Dread"; 10) "The Leopard's Lair"; 11) "The Fire of the Gods"; 12) "Jungle Justice"

THE VANISHING LEGION
(Mascot Pictures Corp.; 1931)

Thanks to the sharp ears of film historian Dr. Bill G. "Buck" Rainey, we find another Karloff performance in a serial. Dr. Rainey identified a disembodied voice—known only as "the Voice"—as belonging to Boris Karloff, in *The Vanishing Legion*.

In one scene, heroic Happy Cardigan (Harry Carey) holds two crooks at gunpoint and discovers a short-wave radio receiver. Cardigan hears: "The Voice speaking! Tonight, we strike at one who has learned too much! Gather at the ranch headquarters at 9 o'clock. The Voice has spoken!"

It was a striking accomplishment for Nat Levine to hire Harry Carey and Edwina Booth—both major stars in MGM's blockbuster hit of 1930, *Trader Horn*—for *The Vanishing Legion*. Perennial child actor Frankie Darro stands out as a kid who fights to prove his father innocent of a murder charge. Miss Booth sometimes appears awkward, but just as often she does a perfectly acceptable job as the spunky heroine. The supporting players, including reliables Lafe McKee and Robert Kortman, generally bring a believability to their roles.

Carey's Happy Cardigan, an oilman and engineer, has been hired to halt sabotage by a vigilante group called The Vanishing Legion. Caroline Hall (Miss Booth), who feels that she has been cheated by the oil company, initially leads the Legion. She blames the slaying of her father upon someone connected to the company. Meanwhile, a gang led by the Voice allows its attacks to be blamed on the Vanishing Legion. Only when Caroline Hall begins to trust Happy Cardigan can the two begin

Harry Carey, Edwina Booth in *The Vanishing Legion.* **(Photofest)**

working together. They realize that another gang is responsible. By teaming with Cardigan, Caroline angers the rest of the Legion, which continues to harass the oil company.

At least one director of the company may be the Voice. Jed Williams (Edward Hearn), once an executive, has been framed for murder by someone on the board. He is helped by his son, Jimmy (Frankie Darro) and by Happy. Jimmy has befriended a wild horse named Rex, who fears men because of abusive former owners. Rex (played by a splendid trained animal named Rex, King of the Wild Horses) will allow only Jimmy to ride him. Lawyer and board member Hornbeck (Lafe McKee) also seems willing to prove Jed's innocence.

The plot device of an unseen villain who uses electrical gadgetry was stock-in-trade for the serials, from the many *Clutching Hand* episodes to *The Whispering Shadow* (1933) and *Ace Drummond* (1936) and beyond.

Cardigan finally corners and exposes the villain, and after a terrific fight it appears that Happy has been knocked out. Before the mastermind can escape, he is trampled to death by Rex.

Harry Carey is perfectly at ease as Happy Cardigan, generating a tremendous sense of quiet authority. Carey is the serial's greatest asset, ably supported by the strong though modest production values and by the on-screen likes of Frankie Darro, Edward Hearn, Bob Kortman and Lafe McKee.

Because we only hear Boris Karloff's voice, his artistry at this point must be judged by his spoken projection and how it conveys the threat of an all-knowing, all-seeing conspiracy. Karloff's voice already has that wonderfully menacing intelligence that helped to make his work over the long haul so memorable.

Karloff was now 43 years old. Despite meatier roles—such as the stage and screen versions of *The Criminal Code*—here he was, still making serials. Meanwhile, Bela Lugosi's future had never looked brighter.

CREDITS: Producer: Nat Levine; Director: B. Reaves [given elsewhere as Reeves] Eason; Screenplay and Story: Wyndham Gittens, Ford Beebe and Helmer Bergman. Photographed by: Ben Kline, Ernest Miller and Jo J. Novak, IATSE; Musical Direction: Lee Zahler; Film Editor: Ray Snyder; Supervising Editor: Wyndham Gittens; Sound Recording: George Lowerre, Disney Film Recording Co.; a Serial in 12 Chapters; Released: June 1, 1931

CAST: Harry Carey (Happy Cardigan); Edwina Booth (Caroline Hall); Rex, King of the Wild Horses (Rex); William Desmond (Sheriff); Frankie Darro (Jimmy Williams); Philo McCullough (Stevens); Yakima Canutt, Dick Dickinson and Joe Bonomo (Riders of the Legion); Tom Dugan (Board Member); Lafe McKee (Hornbeck/the Voice); Bob Kortman (Larno); Edward Hearn (Jed Williams); Frank Brownlee (Bishop); Olive Fuller Golden [Mrs. Harry Carey] (Miss Lewis); Bob Walker (Allen); Al Taylor (Sheriff of Slocum); Pete Morrison (Valenti); Dick Hatton (Dodge); Boris Karloff (Off-screen voice of the Voice); and Paul Wiegel, Charles "Rube" Schaeffer

CHAPTER TITLES: 1) "The Voice from the Void"; 2) "The Queen of the Night Riders"; 3) "The Invisible Enemy"; 4) "The Fatal Message"; 5) "The Trackless Trail"; 6) "The Radio Riddle"; 7) "The Crimson Clue"; 8) "The Doorway of Disaster"; 9) "When Time Stood Still"; 10) "Riding the Whirlwind"; 11) "The Capsule of Oblivion"; 12) "The Hoofs of Horror"

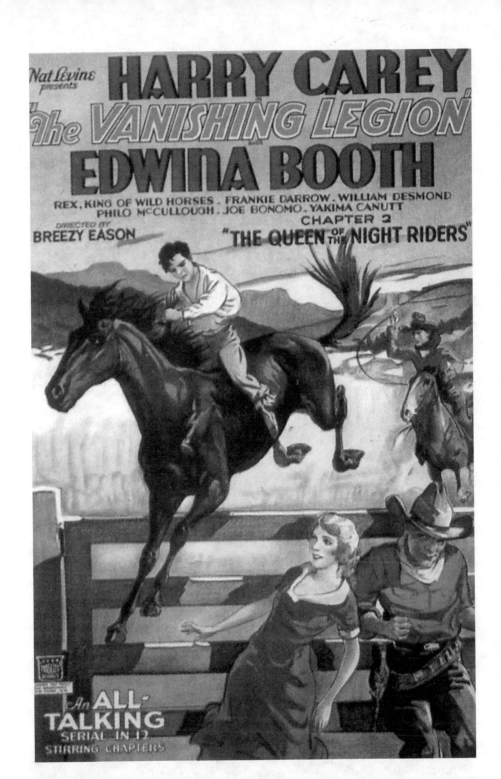

Sinister Serials: Bela Lugosi

CHAPTER FOUR
Hungarian Ghoulish: The Sinister Serials of Bela Lugosi

Not only was Bela Lugosi (1882-1956) larger than life within the literal dimensions of the 20-by-40-foot movie screen, he was larger than life within the constraints of life itself. So thoroughly identified had Lugosi become with the role of Dracula that even in his handful of matinee-serial appearances, as the chapter-play researcher Alan G. Barbour has noted, "One was constantly waiting for the fanged teeth and the accompanying bite-on-the-neck to appear." Many perfectly well-civilized American fans, caught up in the lasting thrall of Lugosi's undead Dracula image, could not help but wonder if the actor's very demise might be a put-on. Comedian Joey Bishop's quip, on hearing the sad news in 1956, was: "He'll be back." Only several years later, Bishop acknowledged the remark but insisted he intended no flippancy. "I meant exactly what I said: 'He'll be back.' Because no presence that majestic, that influential on the cultural psyche, stays gone for long, dead or alive."

Bishop's remark, in a sense, had proved unnervingly accurate. Within scarcely a year of Lugosi's death, the actor's Depression-era Universal pictures would come to syndicated television with all the popular appeal of a network-sweeps original. Soon, the mass audience would create a demand for model kits, posters, greeting cards and Halloween masks bearing the Lugosi likeness, along with the faces of Boris Karloff and Lon Chaney, Jr. The confrontational comedian Lenny Bruce found one of his more crowd-pleasing routines in a caricature of Lugosi. Two impressive biographies, by Arthur Lennig and Robert Cremer, appeared during the 1970s, and Martin Landau won an Oscar for his portrayal of Lugosi in Tim Burton's fanciful bio-picture, *Ed Wood* (1994). Landau, despite an over-written role, found a truer essence of Lugosi in one simple understanding: "In good films or in films beneath his dignity, on camera or stage or just mingling backstage, Lugosi seems to have had a bold, theatrical sense of himself. What a *massive* personality he must have been!" Landau told syndicated film columnist Michael H. Price.

For all the scholarship, image-hawking and gossip that have accumulated around Lugosi's feature-film career, his five movie serials of 1933-39 have gone largely undiscussed. These productions had been difficult to locate until the home-video upheaval of the past generation. In the early days of mass-market television, serials and matinee Westerns flooded the airwaves—as cheap, convenient programming, selected indiscriminately and broadcast likewise, with little sense of showmanship beyond just letting the footage run. Many were played literally to death until only tattered remnants clung to their reels, having been shown without maintenance and given only stopgap repairs on the fly. When television started creating original programming in earnest, the older films were gradually discarded. Surviving television prints languished for years in the storage rooms of small-market independent broadcasting stations and boondocks network affiliates. These, in turn, became a cornerstone of the first-generation home-video market around 1980, when small labels went scrambling for inexpensive titles to supply an unexpected onslaught of videocassette consumerism. Thus have the long-neglected Lugosi serials come haltingly back to light.

Lugosi's zeal, which comes to the fore no matter what the pedigree of the film, is chiefly what makes these raggedy productions worth watching. Perhaps the most perceptive observation on this quality came from the inept filmmaker Edward D. Wood, Jr. as quoted by Wood biographer Rudolph Grey:

> Lugosi... has that beautiful little snickering laugh of his—"*Heh, heh, heh*"—which is not a laugh, it's almost a piece of dialogue. Nobody else could do it. Karloff, Lorre, Greenstreet, it was his....

In the early 1930s, the movie serial was hardly the type of project that most major movie stars would undertake. The old Hollywood saying, "You're only as good as your last picture," was as true then as today. A star who made a string of lesser pictures had to work hard for resurgence. This is what happened to Bela Lugosi.

Bela Lugosi's most famous role, Count Dracula in *Dracula* (1931).

By 1932, Lugosi was coasting on his *Dracula* fame, like it or not. Boris Karloff had now eclipsed him as a major star at Universal. Even so, Lugosi's name was still big at the box-office. Although Lugosi had appeared in two independent productions, the runaway hit fantasy *White Zombie* (1932) and the murder-in-Hollywood mystery *The Death Kiss*

(1933), these were not generally regarded as low-budget films. *White Zombie* was given the prestige of a United Artists release, and *The Death Kiss* was issued through Fox. Lugosi had key supporting roles at Paramount, in *International House* (opposite W.C. Fields) and *Island of Lost Souls* (opposite Charles Laughton) in 1933. Lugosi's only real lapse of strategic judgment was a red-herring role in Columbia's disappointing *Night of Terror*, that same year. Bankruptcy proceedings plagued the actor during 1933—the worst year of the Depression—but Lugosi had seemed to be living well just the previous year. Remarkably youthful-looking at nearly 50 when he was interviewed on film by reporter Dorothy West for the short-subject series *Intimate Interviews*, Lugosi clearly was enjoying his fame as the country's pre-eminent bogeyman. In one segment, Lugosi displays a sardonic sense of humor:

"Do you believe in vampires?" asks Miss West. Lugosi replies, "Yes," and then pauses before adding: "*Three* of them, I *married!*"

A Los Angeles newspaper account from late 1932 finds Lugosi filing for bankruptcy, listing $2,495 in liabilities and only $600 in ready assets. A former housekeeper had filed an additional wage claim for $700. In early 1933, Lugosi was sued for a $700 arrearage in rent on an apartment.

Lugosi eventually paid off his debts, saved his money despite his tastes for fine dining, expensive cigars and generous tipping, and hired a secretary to help with his financial affairs. The secretary, Lillian Arch, was more than 20 years younger than Bela, but she was likewise of Hungarian descent and there was a mutual attraction. Miss Arch soon became the fourth Mrs. Bela Lugosi.

Lugosi had been accustomed to the good life for many years. Once a major star on the Hungarian stage, he experienced his first financial setbacks when he was forced to flee Hungary after the Communist revolution in 1921. Stowing away aboard an Italian freighter bound for the United States, Lugosi arrived in America penniless and ill versed in the English language. Lugosi wrote in a bylined article for the promotional book accompanying 1934's *The Return of Chandu*:

> In the Greek language, the terms stranger,
> or foreigner, and enemy are identical. It is
> assumed that a foreigner must be a bar-
> barian and foe. A little of that sentiment

endures to this day. At least I found it so, coming to America from Hungary. Though it is egotism, it is, I hope, pardonable when an artist has achieved recognition in his own country, to take it for granted that his name is not entirely strange in other centers of culture, and perhaps to resent it when he finds out that he is quite unknown and must begin again, as you say in this elegant country, from scratch.

Money was only one of Lugosi's worries in 1933. His Universal contract had called for only one more picture after *Dracula*. Universal planned *Frankenstein* as this next picture and announced Lugosi as the Monster.

However, Lugosi made it known that he did not want to play such a brutish monster, especially one that could not talk! Director Robert Florey was experiencing budgetary problems and creative differences with the studio. *Frankenstein* was then assigned to director James Whale. While Lugosi continued to grumble about playing the Monster, James Whale discovered Boris Karloff. Lugosi's refusal to play the Monster may have caused ill feelings with long-term repercussions. The role of a lifetime went to Karloff, whom Bela Lugosi often called "my rival."

Murders in the Rue Morgue (1932) became the consolation prize for both

Robert Florey and Bela Lugosi. The film was based on the Edgar Allan Poe story, with Lugosi playing his first of many mad scientists, Dr. Mirakle. Florey structured and paced the film as if remaking *The Cabinet of Dr. Caligari* (1919). A popular theory holds that Universal felt the film too fancy and re-edited it against Florey's wishes. However, Florey's bigorapher Brian Taves has found no evidence of any post-production tampering. By comparison with *Frankenstein*, the Poe takeoff fared poorly at the box-office. Robert Florey left the studio. Bela Lugosi would not return until *The Black Cat* in 1934.

Lugosi was now a free-lance actor, free to choose his assignments but cut loose from his corporate moorings. Had Universal signed him as a contract player, Lugosi would have received a careful build-up and a chance to have star vehicles tailored to him—as would become Karloff's lot after *Frankenstein*. Unfortunately, Lugosi too often let his agents and his under-stuffed wallet decide what parts he should play. Lillian Lugosi Donlevy explained to biographer Robert Cremer:

> Bela's biggest problem [was] that he left everything to his agents. That is one of the reasons why he passed up the part of the Frankenstein monster. He had a stupid agent at the time. If his agent had been at all clever, he would have calmed Bela down and then pointed out that he was tops in the field since the death of Lon Chaney, Sr. Of course, it only stood to reason that Bela shouldn't introduce his own competition, but his agent didn't understand that. If he had, there might never have been a Karloff in the field.

Bela Lugosi now had a rival in Boris Karloff, whose starring picture *The Mummy* (1932) proved similar in concept to *Dracula*—but far superior in cinematic terms. Karloff, now a major star at Universal, managed his money well and even walked out on his contract when he felt underpaid or overworked. This was one of the concerns that led Karloff and Lugosi to help establish the Screen Actors Guild. Remembering what had happened to protesting actors in Hungary, Lugosi kept a low profile

in SAG for a few years, but was an active member. Lugosi identified sharply with the working class and was not much for idle socializing with the more privileged classes.

Lugosi, unlike Karloff, was shy around people he didn't know. We can ascribe this to his problems in learning the idiosyncrasies of the English language, and to his absorption in giving a good performance, rather than fraternizing with the other cast members around him. The fact that Lugosi rarely got to know the people he worked with, particularly in the 1930s, can only have hurt his career. Most of the Hollywood stars tended to socialize with each other. Much business was done at social occasions, but Lugosi in the early years was a lone wolf in Hollywood. Some stars found him aloof, others who made the point of getting to know him better found him to be a charming, dedicated artist. Of course, not everyone took the time to find this out, and many people in the industry tended to judge Lugosi's dramatic worth by the false yardstick of the mismanagement of his career. One such misstep in a greater career strategy was *The Whispering Shadow*, which to many people indelibly branded Lugosi a lapsed major-leaguer turned serial hack.

THE WHISPERING SHADOW
(Mascot Pictures Corp.; 1933)

Inside Professor Anton Strang's wax museum, two figures confront one another. The younger man is Jack Foster (Malcolm McGregor), whose transfer and storage company is under attack by a terrorist group headed by a mystery man known as the Whispering Shadow. Foster accuses Professor Strang (Bela Lugosi) of being the master criminal.

Sinister Serials: Bela Lugosi

What could have prompted Lugosi to lower himself to star in a movie serial? It would be too easy to say he did so only for the money. Producer Nat Levine, in several late-in-life interviews, said that Lugosi was paid $10,000 for the indulgence. "The pleasure was all ours," Levine told Michael H. Price during the 1960s, "and we cut Bela as good a deal as we'd cut for any name player." Most of Mascot's serials were turned out in a brisk three weeks, and a salary of over $3,000 a week was very good money. George E. Turner has maintained that *The Whispering Shadow* represented a sound financial move on Lugosi's part: "Good move, for a couple of weeks' work—more [money] than most big contract stars made at the major studios."

It is a mystery, all the same, as to just what caused Lugosi to lapse from major stardom in scarcely more than a year. Universal's comparative stinginess may be a factor here, and passive representation in the talent-agent department must also be considered. Hints of a Universal blacklisting (official or otherwise) cannot be ignored, but one key researcher, Brian Taves, reports no evidence of trouble between Lugosi and Universal in light of the actor's refusal to follow through with *Frankenstein* (1931).

Then, too, Lugosi spent much of the early '30s as a co-founder of the Screen Actors Guild. As Don Ameche told Mike Price in a 1986 interview: "What Bela *really* ought to be remembered for, is that he put his neck on the block as one of the main unionizers of our profession—not just the acting profession, but for all of us who labored before and behind the cameras. Management preferred its stars *un*-organized, and Bela took a very courageous stance, there. No grandstanding, because he knew better than to call attention to himself. But a sustained act of courage, it was, indeed, on Bela's part."

Boris Karloff voiced his own theories in a radio interview with Colin Edwards, c. 1960:

> He had a tragic, tragic life, that man... I've
> always felt extremely sorry for him. In a
> way, he was his own worst enemy. He was
> a fine actor. He was a brilliant technician,
> a brilliant technician, in every sense of the
> word, but he hadn't moved with the times.
> He was the leading man, I believe, in the

Viva Tattersall plays the daughter of Professor Strang (Lugosi) in *The Whispering Shadow*.

state theater, I think in Budapest, when he was a young man, with a fine, fine, European sort of reputation, but, he just didn't move with the times. And when he came to America, he didn't learn the language as well as he might have. I'm afraid that those things were bad for him.

Whatever the reasons, Lugosi was unsure of his stardom, and of his finances. *The Whispering Shadow* can only have struck him as a winning situation.

Lugosi plays Professor Anton Strang—a "sinister being," according to a title card—who operates a wax museum while practicing magic and electrical experiments on the side. If any of Lugosi's performances can be called bombastic, it is certainly this one, even though there is hardly much depth about the character or the actor's reading of it. Ford Beebe,

Jr. has brought up an enlightening point about the rigors of serial making, which render dramatic weight almost beside the point:

> When you've got a schedule of close to 100 scenes a day how are you [the director] going to sit there and say [to a cast member], "I don't really think you've put enough feeling into the scene"—?

When Mascot Pictures was forcibly merged into Republic Studios, later in the '30s, the new studio wisely retained what was good about the Mascot serials—the relentless action—and improved upon the weak spots of pacing, character and musical scoring. Mascot historian Jon Tuska hails the little studio's "emphasis on hectic activity," which "compensated for the spiritual lethargy of the times."

The Whispering Shadow is brimming with suspicious characters, including a particularly hammy villain known as Alexis Steinbeck, played by Roy D'Arcy of 1928's *The Merry Widow*. Lee Zahler's main-title music is majestic as well as mysterious, promising far more than the serial comes prepared to deliver. This Zahler composition turns up in several later films. Other *Whispering Shadow* music comes from Abe Meyer's company, Meyer Synchronizing Service, a vast library of stock scores.

Professor Strang is up to no good in this scene from *The Whispering Shadow*.

Much of the serial is set around the trucking company, and effective use is made of Los Angeles' huge Bekins warehouse. The serial excels as an inadvertent document of early 1930s Southern California, with dusty roads and wide-open spaces.

The Whispering Shadow was directed by Albert Herman and Colbert "Bert" Clark. Despite Clark's growing expertise, the acting is stiff and overdone. The special effects ranged from good to awful. Barney Sarecky, Wyndham Gittens and Norman S. Hall were veteran serial scenarists, and they all would work, at one time or another, on the *Flash Gordon* trilogy. Sarecky would meet Lugosi again as associate producer on a terrible series of Monogram low-budgeters during the 1940s.

Shadow's comic relief is entrusted to a character called Sparks, a seemingly dimwitted employee at the trucking company, who is often

If any of Lugosi's performances can be called bombastic, it is certainly Professor Strang in *The Whispering Shadow*.

seen fumbling with a strange wire toy. Originally, Mascot had hired the pioneering silent-screen comedian Harry Langdon, now down on his luck, but the part finally fell to Karl Dane, a Danish comedian well known in silent films. Dane's heavy accent kept him largely idled in the talking pictures, and *Shadow* marked his last performance. In 1934, Dane committed suicide. Backup players Henry B. Walthall and Bob Kortman also were veterans of silent films. Viva Tattersall, who plays Vera Strang, was the wife of Sidney Toler, who himself was several years away from inheriting the role of Charlie Chan at 20th Century-Fox.

In 1933, Universal Studios was considering starring Lugosi with Karloff in a sequel to *Frankenstein*, to be called *The Return of Frankenstein*. The project became, of course, *Bride of Frankenstein* (1935)— minus Lugosi. However, the idea of teaming the artists remained vital, and Universal signed Lugosi to appear opposite Karloff in *The Black Cat* (1934). There were innumerable script problems, and while Lugosi waited, he got an offer from Sol Lesser's Principal Pictures to appear in *The Return of Chandu*.

CREDITS: Producer: Nat Levine; Directors: Albert Herman and Colbert Clark; Story: Barney Sarecky, George Morgan, Norman S. Hall, Colbert Clark and Wyndham Gittens; Photography: Ernest Miller and Edgar Lyons; Supervising Editor: Wyndham Gittens; Film Editors: Ray Snyder and Gilmore Walker; Sound Engineer: Homer Ackerman; Sound: International Recording Engineers; Production Manager: Larry Wickland; Associate Producer: Victor Zobel; Continuity: Howard Bimberg; Operative Cameraman: Victor Scheurich; Assistant Directors, George Webster and Theodore "Doc" Joos; Cutter: George Halligan; Sound Supervisor: Terry Kellum; Musical Direction: Abe Meyer; a Serial in 12 Chapters; Also Released in a Six-Reel Feature Version; Released: January 15, 1933

CAST: Bela Lugosi (Professor Anton Strang); Viva Tattersall (Vera Strang); Malcolm McGregor (Jack Foster); Henry B. Walthall (President Bradley); Robert Warwick (Detective Raymond); Ethel Clayton (The Countess); Roy D'Arcy (Steinbeck); Karl Dane (Sparks); Lloyd Whitlock (Young); Bob Kortman (Slade); Lafe McKee (Jerome); George J. Lewis (Bud Foster); Jack Perrin (Williams); Max Wagner (Kruger); Kernan Kripps (Foreman); Eddie Parker (Driver); Gordon De Main (Detective); George Magrill (Mitchell); Tom London (Dupont); Lionel Backus (Jarvis); Norman Frasier (Deane)

CHAPTER TITLES: 1) "The Master Magician"; 2) "The Collapsing Room"; 3) "The All-Seeing Eye"; 4) "The Shadow Strikes"; 5) "Wanted for Murder"; 6) "The Man Who Was Czar"; 7) "The Double Room"; 8) "The Red Circle"; 9) "The Fatal Secret"; 10) "The Death Warrant"; 11) "The Trap"; 12) "King of the World"

THE RETURN OF CHANDU
(Principal Pictures Corp.; 1934)

It is a tense moment for Frank Chandler (Bela Lugosi), also known as the heroic magician, Chandu. His beloved, Princess Nadji, has been kidnapped by the evil Vindhyan. Chandu confronts the knife-wielding villain, and a battle of wills is struck. "Drop that knife!" Chandu orders, staring intently into Vindhyan's hypnotic gaze. "Drop—that—knife! *Drop*! *That*! *Knife*!" The knife slowly falls from Vindhyan's fingers.

Chandu originated with a radio program in 1932 over California-based Station KHJ. Fox Film Corp. seized upon the character's big-screen possibilities, and by the time a feature-film version had been completed, the Mutual Radio Network had begun playing the program nationwide.

Bela Lugosi graced Fox's 1932 *Chandu the Magician* as a bad guy named Roxor, opposite Edmund Lowe's imperson-ation of Chandu. The popu-larity of the film and the ra-dio serial led independent producer Sol Lesser to tackle a serial version two years later, with Fox's bless-ing. Lesser got an inspira-tion: Instead of furthering Lugosi's typecasting with another villainous role, he would cast Lugosi as the he-roic magician. Promotional materials quote Lesser to the effect that Lugosi's voice "visualizes [*sic*] Chandu perfectly," and that "[Lugosi's] skill as an actor could be depended upon to complete visualization of what Chandu looks, acts

Tyba (Joseph Swickard) tries to free Chandu (Lugosi) in *The Return of Chandu*.

and talks like." The production began in mid-July 1934 and wrapped up in a generous five weeks.

The story concerns Dr. Frank "Chandu" Chandler's romance with the beautiful Egyptian princess, Nadji (Maria Alba). Nadji is menaced by a cult known as the Ubasti. On the cult's well-protected island of Lemuria reposes the preserved body of the Ubastis' ancient ruler, Ossana. The cultists believe that the soul of Nadji can revive Ossana. Chandu will need all his powers to save the day.

Lugosi seems overjoyed to be playing a romantic hero. Now nearly 52 years old and saddled with the task of playing a character some 20 years younger, he does so to near-perfection.

Historian George E. Turner was constantly annoyed when he read past and contemporary reviews regarding the hero Frank Chandler known as Chandu. George stated that the radio show, which began in 1932, was a serialized adventure program for children. Chandu was not the young pugnacious two-fisted he-man hero. He was approaching middle age

Chandu uses hypnotism to subdue a Ubasti cult member in *The Return of Chandu.*

and was a peace-loving bachelor who adored his sister Dorothy's teen-aged children. Chandu had studied the mystical secrets and philosophy of the East Orient. While Chandu was every bit as adventurous as Flash Gordon, John Wayne or Buck Jones, he used his mind rather than his fists to extract himself from dangerous situations. He continually seeks the help from his wise old teacher or yogi.

Many reviewers considered the character weak for this very reason. What the reviewers fail to realize, Turner explained, was that Chandu was supposed to be an ordinary man who had some extraordinary powers that must be used wisely, not blindly, in the heat of action.

Many episodes of the recycled 1948-1950 radio version of *Chandu* are available for fans to enjoy. The changes, other than cast, were few although recent events such as WWII were added by writer Vera Oldham, who along with Harry A. Earnshaw and R.R. Morgan authored the 1932 version. Director Cyril Armbrister, the original radio director, helmed the 1948 remake. A close audio comparison between the three actors

Lugosi at his most heroic in *The Return of Chandu*.

who portrayed Chandu (Edmund Lowe, Bela Lugosi and Tom Collins) confirms Turner's theory that Chandu was a nice guy who happened to be a magician.

The Return of Chandu is essential viewing for Lugosi fans. The 12-chapter serial, despite its flaws, enables Lugosi to return to the heroic roles he had performed on stage before *Dracula*.

Veteran silent-screen player Wilfred Lucas plays the bedraggled captain of the rescue ship. Castilian actress and dancer Maria Alba is charming and believable as Princess Nadji. Clara Kimball Young, a silent-film actress and former entrepreneurial producer who had seen better days, is good as Chandu's sister. Lucien Prival plays a particularly nasty villain.

The musical scoring is extraordinarily effective, taking full advantage of Abe Meyer's library of superbly preserved canned dramatic cues, including Nem Herkan's "S.O.S." and "In the Depths"; "Impatience," by Milan Roder; and a re-orchestration of Kristof W. Gluck's "The Dance of the Furies," from the second revised production of the opera *Orfeo é Euridice* of 1774. These are but a few of the exciting and familiar themes that course through the serial.

Lesser also made strategic use of found objects in the properties department: There can be seen sets from *King Kong* (1933), particularly the Great Wall and its colossal gate; and sets from *The Son of Kong* (1933) and *The King of Kings* (1927).

Lesser offered theater owners either the 12 chapters of the serial or a hybrid feature-plus-serial version. Here, the first four chapters were carefully edited into a feature, also entitled *The Return of Chandu*, to be followed by the remaining eight chapters. For theaters that wanted only features, Lesser had the remaining chapters cut into a short-order sequel called *Chandu on the Magic Island*.

In an Internet discussion involving several fans of Lugosi's work, Father Michael Paraniuk of Ohio made an interesting observation about *The Return of Chandu*: "Remember in *Star Wars* where Obi tells Luke Skywalker to trust the Force which helps him to use his Jedi sword to defeat the evil Darth Vader? In *Chandu*, Bela talks to the 'Teacher' who tells him not to be afraid and 'have faith.' Bela lets go of the steering wheel of the car. The 'Teacher' (substitute 'Force') miraculously guides the car to the evil High Priest's house, where Bela rescues the Egyptian Princess Nadji from certain death... [Y]ears before *Star Wars*..., Bela was already 'using the Force'!"

In a similar light, it bears noting that this 1934 chapter play's subplot about soul transference was appropriated for a crucial scene in Universal Pictures' 1999 remake-of-sorts of *The Mummy*.

Location shot from *The Return of Chandu*

Film historian William K. Everson once wrote that Lugosi played Chandu "as though he were not convinced that he wouldn't turn out to be the villain after all in the final chapter." Everson told me in 1995 that he took this perception directly from a conversation with Lugosi—who said he was not always sure of how to play Chandu and received little help from director Ray Taylor.

Following the success of *The Black Cat* in 1934, Bela Lugosi signed a three-picture deal with Universal. These films would be *The Raven* (1935), *The Invisible Ray* (1936) and *Postal Inspector* (1936). *Cat*, *Raven* and *Ray* are all fine teamings, but *The Raven* is anomalous in that it has the look and feel of a high-class movie serial. For starters, *The Raven* was directed by Louis Friedlander (1901-1962), later known as Lew Landers. Friedlander had become a specialist in serials at Universal, with

Frank Chandler rescues Princess Nadji (Maria Alba) in *The Return of Chandu*.

the likes of *Tailspin Tommy* and *The Vanishing Shadow* (both 1934). *The Raven*, as Friedlander's first feature assignment, is paced and cut in a wonderfully serial-like fashion.

Lugosi gives a superbly wicked performance as Dr. Vollin in *The Raven*, and plays the benevolent scientist Dr. Benet extremely well in *The Invisible Ray*. The last film in his Universal deal from the middle 1930s, *Postal Inspector*—a strange amalgam of gangster melodrama,

comedy and musical—finds Lugosi playing a shady nightclub owner, pursued by the heroic title character, Ricardo Cortez. Although Lugosi has a good part, *Postal Inspector* is clearly a throwaway for Universal. No doubt the encroaching new regime at Universal Pictures, sensing the British-European rumblings that would erupt in 1937 in an international ban on horrific pictures, wanted to get rid of their pioneering horror star and saddled him with *Postal Inspector* to put paid to his contract. Universal management pulled the same ploy on Boris Karloff with *Night Key* in 1937. Early in 1937, Hollywood stopped making horror films as a matter of industrial policy. It was the end of an era, and nearly the end of Lugosi's career.

CREDITS: Producer: Sol Lesser; Director: Ray Taylor. Supervisor: Frank Melford; Adapted from the Radio Drama Created by: Harry A. Earnshaw, Vera M. Oldham and R.R. Morgan; Adaptation and Screenplay: Barry Barringer; Story Supervisor: Harry Chandlee, by Arrangement with Jesse L. Lasky; Photographed by John Hickson; Production Manager: Theodore Joos; Musical Director: Abe Meyer; Art Director: Robert Ellis; Dialogue Director: Cyril Armbrister; Film Editors: Carl Himm and Lou Sackin; Sound Recording: Corson Jowett; Assistant Director: Harry Knight; a Serial in 12 Chapters, 24 reels; Running Time: 214 minutes; Released: October 1, 1934, via Fox Film Corp. The serial was later edited as a two-part feature—*The Return of Chandu* (1934) and *Chandu on the Magic Island* (1935).

CAST: Bela Lugosi (Frank Chandler/Chandu); Maria Alba (Princess Nadji); Clara Kimball Young (Dorothy Regent); Lucien Prival (Vindhyan); Deane Ben-ton (Bob Regent); Phyllis Ludwig (Betty Regent); Cyril Armbrister (Sutra); Murdoch MacQuarrie (the Voice); Wilfred Lucas (Captain Wilson); Josef Swickard (Tyba, the White Magician); Jack Clark (Vitras); Bryant Washburn (Prince Andra); Peggy Montgomery (Judy); Elias Lazaroff (Bara); Dick Bottiler (Morta); Frazer Acosta (Nito); Harry Walker (Tagora); Charles Meacham (Mr. James); Isobel LeMall (Mrs. James); Don Brodie (Reporter); Edward Piel

(Airline Agent); Henry Hall (Curator); Beatrice Roberts (Lady); Iron Eyes Cody (Cat Man); Elias Schaffer (Old Man); Merrill McCormick (Sacrificial Man); Beatrice Roberts and Gloria Holden (Party Guests)

CHAPTER TITLES: 1) "The Chosen Victim"; 2) "The House on the Hill"; 3) "On the High Seas"; 4) "The Evil Eye"; 5) "The Invisible Circle"; 6) "Chandu's False Step"; 7) "The Mysterious Island"; 8) "The Edge of the Pit"; 9) "The Invisible Terror"; 10) "The Crushing Rock"; 11) "The Uplifted Knife"; 12) "The Knife Descends"

SHADOW OF CHINATOWN
(Victory Pictures Corp.; 1936)

After finishing *The Invisible Ray* at Universal, Lugosi was hired for an espionage mystery, *The House of a Thousand Candles*, at Republic Pictures. He fell ill early on and was replaced in the spymaster role by Irving Pichel. This was unfortunate for Lugosi, not just because of a lost opportunity but because Republic seemed to treat its stock-in-trade bad-guy actors very well. Over the years, Lugosi's agents advised him to sign contracts for limited attachments to any given studio, rather than be tied down to a studio for a fixed term. This gave the actor freedom of choice—providing, of course, that one studio or another would present an opportunity in Lugosi's line of specialization. Meanwhile, Boris Karloff had become a salaried, contracted regular at Warners, whose "B"-

Victor Poten (Lugosi) explains the effects of a chemical in *Shadow of Chinatown*.

for-budget unit assured Karloff of a steady run of assignments. No studio had such an obligation to Bela Lugosi, whose roles became fewer and farther between. When he received a call to star in one of Sam Katzman's low-rent independent productions, Lugosi was in no financial shape to refuse.

Katzman had an almost magical knack for knowing how to deliver saleable pictures for the least amount of money. In October 1936, Lugosi began his third serial, *Shadow of Chinatown*, the first of only two serials that Sam Katzman's Victory Pictures would make. Co-featured actor Bruce Bennett—still known in 1936 as Herman Brix—offered this impression of Lugosi to biographer Richard Bojarski:

> ...Lugosi...tried hard to do as convincing a job of playing the role as possible. My general impression of him as a person was that he was rather indrawn—introspective, but his relations with the cast were good.

Shadow of Chinatown was Lugosi's first film for Katzman. The actor should have quit while he was ahead; it's by far the best work that he would do under the Katzman banner. Here, Lugosi plays Victor Poten, a twisted scientist of Asian and European parentage. An outcast from both cultures, Poten seeks a nebulous, sweeping revenge with the help of a fellow Eurasian, the beautiful Sonya Rokoff (played by Luana Walters). Novelist Martin Andrews (played by Herman Brix) and a friend, Willy Fu (Maurice Liu), become embroiled in the intrigues. Growing repentant, Sonya Rokoff tries to escape. Poten cares not that innocent people may be killed in his wave of terrorism.

Top-heavy with plot devices though the serial is, we are never shown an example of the prejudices that have driven

Lugosi creates a fascinatingly conflicted character in *Shadow of Chinatown*.

Poten to madness, although there is a glimpse of this in the dealings between Sonya Rokoff and the various Chinese merchants. It is unusual in this genre that the Chinese community is not held up to ridicule—and that Maurice Liu's character is given some depth and personality.

The screenplay is the work of Isadore Bernstein, author of *Our People* and a former managing director at Universal. Basil Dickey, who also worked on the story, is probably best known to serial fans for his work on the *Flash Gordon* serials. Director Robert S. Hill was a veteran of serials and Westerns, a well-regarded director from the silent-movie days and a former associate of the great German director Paul Leni. Hill would later co-direct *Flash Gordon's Trip to Mars* (1938) with Ford Beebe. A standout among the supporting cast is Charlie King, a favorite villain from the Western shoot-'em-up sector. Here, King plays one of Lugosi's henchmen, whose disloyalty earns him the privilege of being transformed into a zombie.

Lugosi creates a fascinatingly conflicted character, a sadistic fiend who seems to grow more ruthless with each new scheme. Luana Walters is a rare beauty, and a competent player who convincingly delineates a villain who experiences a change of heart. Miss Walters would meet Lugosi again—with a better performance, but in a terrible film—in Katzman's 1942 production of *The Corpse Vanishes*. Former Olympic swimmer Herman Brix is a likable hero, recalling the charismatic presence of Buster Crabbe, if Crabbe had possessed a big-nosed profile. Joan Barclay, in a secondary heroic/endangered role, delivers an uneven portrayal. George Turner once described Miss Barclay's overall acting style as that of "a society girl gone slumming." Miss Barclay had been a contract player at Warner Bros., but once she wound up working for Sam Katzman she never escaped the low-budget ranks.

Miss Barclay plays a society columnist who longs to become a crusading reporter. The proto-feminist angle notwithstanding, her role is compromised by an overabundance of comic relief. At one point, the character uses real wit and intelligence, but elsewhere she acts like a scatterbrain. As a saving grace, Miss Barclay and Brix convey a strong chemistry. The actor playing Brix's friend, Maurice Liu, was a filmmaker representing the Chinese government, newly arrived in America to study cinematography.

The unattributed main-title music, a mys-

Poten uses various disguises in his quest for evil in *Shadow of Chinatown*.

terious mock-Oriental motif, is striking, but the incidental background music is uninspired. The occasional visual effect—such as the pages of an exotic-looking book, slowly turning to reveal photos of the cast—lends a classy touch. The fight scenes and special effects are adequate, but nowhere near the standards set by Republic Studios' early serials of the same period.

Because the company worked as quickly and cheaply as possible, the serial has an off-the-cuff look, almost as if shot in documentary fashion. *Shadow of Chinatown* is in some respects a better-looking product than one would expect from Sam Katzman.

By the time Bela Lugosi had finished *Shadow of Chinatown*, Universal Pictures had been sold to a new group of investors. Not only were studio chief Carl Laemmle, Sr. and his chief personnel—including many Laemmle kin—ousted, but all pending productions and undeveloped story

Charlie King doesn't know that his boss knows exactly what he is up to.

properties were shelved, especially the prospective horror films. The final blow came from Great Britain's Board of Censors, which began slapping all films of this genre with the dreaded "H" certificate, an adults-only flag, as a prelude to an international ban. Hollywood, spooked by the collapse of the lucrative Euro-British market for scare-shows, declared the horror film a defunct commodity. Within the U.S. filmmaking establishment, only the serials and a few sub-Poverty Row feature-filmmakers would exhibit the gumption to defy the ban.

CREDITS: Producer: Sam Katzman. Director: Robert S. Hill; Story: Rock Hawkey; Continuity: Isadore Bernstein and Basil Dickey; Special Dialogue: William Buchanan; Photographed by: Walter Hyer; Production Manager: Ed W. Rote; Film Editor: Charles Hinkel; Settings: Fred Preble; Sound Recording; Hans Weeren; a Serial in 15 Chapters, 31 Reels; Feature Version, Running Time: 65 Minutes; Released: October 10, 1936

Willy Fu (Maurice Lu) is captured by Poten in *Shadow of Chinatown*.

CAST: Bela Lugosi (Victor Poten); Herman Brix (Martin Andrews); Luana Walters (Sonya Rokoff); Joan Barclay (Joan Whiting); Maurice Liu (Willy Fu); Charles King (Grogan); William Buchanan (Healy); Forrest Taylor (Captain Walters); James B. Leong (Wong); Henry F. Tung (Dr. Wu); Paul Fung (Tom Chu); George Chan (Old Luee); John Elliot (Captain); Moy Ming (Wong's Brother); Jack Cowell (White Chink) and Lester Dorr, Henry Hall, Roger Williams and Denver Dixon

CHAPTER TITLES: 1) "The Arms of the God"; 2) "The Crushing Walls"; 3) "13 Ferguson Alley"; 4) "Death on the Wire"; 5) "The Sinister Ray"; 6) "The Sword Thrower"; 7) "The Noose"; 8) "Midnight"; 9) "The Last Warning"; 10) "The Bomb"; 11) "Thundering Doom"; 12) "Invisible Gas"; 13) "The Brink of Disaster"; 14) "The Fatal Trap"; 15) "The Avenging Powers"

S O S COAST GUARD
(Republic Pictures Corp.; 1937)

The Coast Guard has been alerted that a spy and inventor known as Boroff has developed a powerful disintegrating gas. Guardsman Terry Kent (Ralph Byrd) is particularly anxious to capture Boroff, who has murdered Terry's brother. Kent is aided by spunky reporter Jean Norman (Maxine Doyle) and her photographer, Snapper (a comic relief role, played by Lee Ford).

Boroff (Bela Lugosi) seems to have things going to quite suit him. He now decides to remove his beard, hoping the altered appearance will help him dodge justice. Thorg (Richard Alexander), Boroff's brutish and ill-treated flunky, wields the razor. We see many conflicting emotions reflected in Thorg's face. Boroff is in control of the situation, however:

"Thorg would like to cut my throat. Wouldn't you, Thorg?" asks Boroff. An accomplice, watching, says, "And why shouldn't he? He's never forgiven you for mutilating his mind!" Boroff finds the scenario amusing: "Go ahead, Thorg! Cut my throat!"

This scene inspired a similar shaving scene between Professor Moriarty (George Zucco) and his servant Dawes (Frank Dawson) in *The Adventures of Sherlock Holmes* in 1939.

SOS *COAST GUARD*

A REPUBLIC PICTURE

Boris Karloff had strategically landed in a safe harbor as a character actor at Warners during this dry spell for horror movies. Lugosi had a strong role in the play *Tovarich* at the Curran Theatre in San Francisco, but made only one film, *S O S Coast Guard*, during 1937. *Tovarich* would be adapted to the screen later that year at Warner Bros., with the big studio's own contracted stars. Basil Rathbone, Lugosi's future co-star in *Son of Frankenstein* (1939), would play the role Lugosi had handled on stage.

S O S Coast Guard marked only the second serial-helmer assignment for William Witney, co-directing with Alan James. Witney was not one to forget the actors who worked hard to make his job easier: "Dick Alexander and Bela Lugosi. These two old pros were a young director's dream come true," he wrote in his memoirs.

Witney would soon become known as one of Republic's top serial men, and the chapter plays he directed with John English are considered among the best ever. Witney later distinguished himself as a director of feature films, from the classic Western *Helldorado* in 1946, through *The Bonnie Parker Story* and *The Cool and the Crazy* in the 1950s, to *Master of the World* and *Forty Guns to Apache Pass* in the '60s.

Boroff (Bela Lugosi) discusses plans with henchmen Richard Alexander and John Piccori in *SOS Coast Guard*.

S O S Coast Guard served as a quick follow-up to the enormously popular *Dick Tracy* serial (1937), which had been Ralph Byrd's breakthrough assignment. Like Bela Lugosi as Count Dracula, Ralph Byrd became the popular embodiment of Dick Tracy via additional serials, features and even a teleseries. Maxine Doyle's *S O S* character is the type of reporter Joan Barclay should have played in *Shadow of Chinatown*: She is smart, resourceful and far removed from the typical serial heroine of the 1930s. (Witney and Miss Doyle were later married.)

Ford Beebe, Jr. offered a strong general idea of the working conditions and creative climate on a serial:

Bela Lugosi in *SOS Coast Guard*. (Photofest)

Serial scripts were written with the scene cuts, including close-ups, a running shot, whatever. Very specifically, but only in the sense of what happened, not how the person reacted, what his feelings were, how far to carry the development of the character or anything like that. These things were not even mentioned... the writers didn't put down anything in the way of characterization, or like that, except possibly in an accompanying opinion, you know. It had a lot to do with the capability of the cast.

S O S Coast Guard was about the best entertainment that a serial fan could ask for in those days. Musical director Raoul Kraushaar was already fixing in place a practice that would become a Republic Pictures standard. This stroke of genius called for blending a mixture of stock music and newly composed scores. For instance, a few bars of something like Franz Liszt's "Mazeppa" would be used here and there, as well as themes from *The Riot* and *Storm and War* by Charles Dunworth and "Dramatic Andante" by Leon Rosebrook. Music from *Dick Tracy* was also used on *S O S*. Republic's house composers, including Alberto Columbo, William Lava, Karl Hajos and Cy Feuer would later record passages of new music so that the music library could retire its older, overused scores.

S O S derives from a story by Morgan Cox and Ronald Davidson. Barry Shipman and Franklyn Adreon handled the screenplay. Lugosi approaches this serial with a remarkable restraint, particularly in his unnerving scene under the razor with Richard Alexander. The serial allows Lugosi too few such moments. For the most part, Lugosi acts the part of the general lording it over an army of hoodlums, barking orders and steering clear of the mayhem he provokes. This tactic was a cost-cutting move, enabling the company to film many different scenes of Lugosi in the course of a few days. This technique of stockpiling footage also assured that the star player, however far removed from the more violent action, would appear involved throughout the story. Director Witney wrote in his memoirs:

> Bela Lugosi had a heavy accent, Hungarian I think, and he was hard to understand. He was a quiet man, and basically a good actor. He had a set of eyes that seemed to change color from blue to black, and came to work in the finest cashmere suit I'd ever seen.

It was a simple scene. He looked out the window and was to turn to his henchmen and say, 'Quick, out the back door,' and everybody would run out the back door. It was almost 8 o'clock at night. I think we were on the 10th take. It still came out, "Qvik, out zee back yahd." It sounded like *yard*. I said, "Bela, it's a door! Door!" I walked to the door and opened and closed it. "Door, Bela, door!" We tried it again and again it came out "yahd" as they ran out the back door. When he came through the door, he looked at me. "I've got zee mental block," he said.

He did have a sense of humor. We were working at an old pier in Hueneme. There were produce-packing houses and a Mexican settlement nearby. Bela was sitting in a chair, and a bunch of Mexican kids circled him, but not too closely. They jabbered and pointed to him. The only English you could understand was "Dracula." He pointed to one of the kids and made a gesture with his finger to come closer. No one moved. He stood and narrowed his eyes down to slits. "Let me see your throat, little boy." In two seconds all of the kids had stampeded around the corner of the building.

On a purely technical level, *S O S Coast Guard* is the best of all of the Lugosi serials. In its finely choreographed action scenes, stunting and special effects, it is typical of the high production values that prevailed at Republic. The weird effect of images appearing to melt at the onslaught of Lugosi's disintegrating gas is a distinct improvement from the use of the same technique in Mascot's *The Phantom Empire* (1935). The effect was created by blowing up key scenes of the film onto soft, gelatin-like photographs, then slowly heating the images. These melting

photographs were then filmed in slow motion, which made it appear that the landscape was melting.

Lugosi biographer Robert Cremer has characterized *S O S Coast Guard* as "a case study of what had happened to the horror film and mystery melodrama since the advent of the [censors'] moratorium. [Lugosi's] role... lacks the pizzazz of some of his later performances. Republic wanted a marketable product that would not arouse the ire of such self-styled vigilantes as the Daughters of the American Revolution, ever on guard for what they considered to be immoral films."

In a rare tradepaper review of a newly issued serial, *Variety* declared that the *S O S Coast Guard* "is a natural for the urchins, and any adult who wanders in will also be kept at the edge of his seat."

With no follow-up assignment in sight, Lugosi fell upon harder times yet. The proud actor had to sell his house, and he became more profoundly worried when he discovered that his wife, Lillian, was pregnant. She gave birth to their only child, Bela George Lugosi, Jr. on January 5, 1938 at Cedars of Lebanon Hospital. The Motion Picture Relief Fund paid the hospital bill. The star-gawking gossip columnist Louella

Parsons wrote with a voyeuristic zeal of Lugosi's financial problems. Her column, in turn, compromised Lugosi's bargaining power for the role that would launch his great comeback—*Son of Frankenstein* (1939).

CREDITS: Executive Producer: Herbert J. Yates; Producer: Sol C. Siegel; Directors: William Witney and Alan James; Screenplay: Barry Shipman, Franklyn Adreon, Winston Miller and Edward Lynn; Story: Morgan Cox, Ronald Davidson, and Lester Scott; Photographed by: William Nobels; Musical Director: Raoul Kraushaar; Production Supervisor: Robert Beche; Production Manager: Allen Wilson; Supervising Editor: Murray Seldeen; Editors: Helene Turner and Edward Todd; Sound: Terry Kellum, Charles J. Lootens and David J. Bloomberg; Special Effects: Howard Lydecker and Theodore Lydecker; Costumes: Robert Ramsey, Elsie Horowitz; Art Direction: John Victor Mackay; Make-up Supervision: Robert Mark; Casting: Harold Dodds; Set Décor: Morris Braun; Construction Supervisor: Ralph Oberg; Location Manager: John T. Bourke; Optical Effects: Consolidated Film Industries; Sound: RCA Victor High Fidelity; a Serial in 12 Chapters; Released: September 30, 1937

CAST: Ralph Byrd (Terry Kent); Bela Lugosi (Boroff); Maxine Doyle (Jean Norman); Richard Alexander (Thorg); Lee Ford (Snapper McGee); John Piccori (G.A. Rackerby); Lawrence Grant (Rabinisi); Thomas Carr (Jim Kent); Carleton Young (Dodds); Allen Connor (Dick Norman); George Chesebro (L.H. Degado); Ramsy Weeks (Wies); Joe Mack (Captain); Herbert Weber (Belden); Dick Sheldon (Attendant); Robert Walker, Sr. (Black); Gene Marvey (Blake); Eddie Philips, Reed Sheffield, Frank Wayne, Warren Jackson and Dick Scott (Boat Heavies); Herbert Rawlinson (Commander Boyle); Jack Clifford (Carter); Jack Daley (Captain); Tom Ung (Charlie); Lee Frederick (Citizen); King Mojave (Driver); Alexander Leftwich (Foreman); Roy Barcroft (Goebel); Joseph Girard (Green); Curley Dresden, Henry Morris, Vinegar Roan and James Millican (Dock Heavies); Lester Dorr (Intern); Edward Cassidy (Johnson); Jack Roberts (Jones); Earl Bunn, Kit Guard (Kelp Heavies); Frank Ellis (Kelp Worker); Henry Hale (Krohn); Fenton "Duke" Taylor (Leader); Harry Strang (Manager); Charles McMurphy (Mate); Edwin Mordant (Meade); Michael Morgan (Moore); Floyd Criswell (Motorcycle Heavies); Bille Van Every (Operator); Rex Lease (Orderly); Alan Gregg (Payne); Loren Riebe (Pete); Frank Fanning, Frank Meredith and John Guston (Policemen); Pat Mitchell (Radioman); Henry Otho (Sailor); Jerry Frank (Sam); Buddy Roosevelt (Scott); Duke York, Forrest Dillon (Sea Heavies); Jack Ingram (Seaman); Dan Wolheim (Slarsen); Roger Williams (Sloan); Frankie Marvin (Sniper); Robert Dudley (Station master); Audrey Gaye (Supervisor); Richard Beach, Enos "Yakima" Canutt, Teddy Mamgean, Baldy Cooke, Robert J. Wilke, Leon Davidson, Jack Long, Bobbie Koshay, Jerry Larkin, Norwood Edwards and Clark Jennings (Men)

CHAPTER TITLES: 1) "Disaster at Sea"; 2) "Barrage of Death"; 3) "The Gas Chamber"; 4) "The Fatal Shaft"; 5) "The Mystery Ship"; 6) "Deadly Cargo"; 7) "Undersea Terror"; 8) "The Crash"; 9) "Wolves at Bay"; 10) "The Acid Trail"; 11) "The Sea Battle"; 12) "The Deadly Circle" A 69 minute feature was released on April 16, 1942.

THE PHANTOM CREEPS
(Universal Pictures Corp.; 1939)

"And now, as the Phantom, there is nothing that I cannot do!" So boasts the bitter, vindictive scientist, Dr. Alex Zorka (Bela Lugosi) to anyone who dares to challenge him. Dr. Zorka has shown his latest invention—a process that can create a state of controlled suspended animation on any living thing—to his wife, Ann (Dora Clement). She is the only person who the scientist will trust completely. Zorka's estranged colleague, Dr. Fred Mallory (Edwin Stanley), has sneaked into the house and witnessed the demonstration:

"It's too bad that Mallory is not here to see my *tri*umph!" exults Zorka.

Mallory interrupts: "I have seen it!"

Zorka is enraged: "You! You—were—*spy*ing!"

"Call it that if you wish, Alex! But you made no secret of it. Now my fear is, what are you going to do with it?"

Dr. Zorka (Lugosi) demonstrates his deadly inventions along with his "snickering laugh" to the terrified Monk (Jack C. Smith) in *The Phantom Creeps*.

"I shall do with it as I *wish*!" replies Zorka, indignantly. "Not hand it over to the government, as *you* would have me!"

"I still think that would be best! It should be under control, for the good of mankind. You would still receive credit for its discovery."

"They would de*stroy* it, if they could!"

"But possibly —"

"*Never* will I let it go! Already, a foreign government has offered me *mill*ions for it…"

Mallory pleads with Zorka: "Don't you realize what a terrific weapon it would be in the hands of unscrupulous people?"

"Of *course*! That is why they shall pay me *dear*ly for it!"

Mrs. Zorka interrupts: "Alex, you must not!"

Mallory: "Then it is my duty to inform the government at once!"

Ann: (Ann sees her husband almost lunge at Mallory) "Alex! Please!"

Zorka regards his wife thoughtfully, then calms down. "All right," he tells Mallory. "If it is your duty, do so by all means, but you will find it a great mis*take*!"

Zorka and Monk observe the spies' headquarters in *The Phantom Creeps*.

"What do you mean?" asks Mrs. Zorka.

The scientist gives a classic Lugosi chuckle, then ends the argument: "You shall soon learn! *All* of you!"

The year 1938 had seen a revival of the horror film as a class, and of Bela Lugosi's career in particular. Beverly Hills' independent Regina Theatre had presented a dual bill of 1931's *Dracula* and *Frankenstein*, tapping a popular demand that gradually provoked an official reissue by Universal. Universal, in due time, commissioned a sequel, *Son of Frankenstein*, and the industry at large finally realized it needed no censor-crazy British-European market to cash in on scary pictures.

Universal was fully aware of Lugosi's financial position. He had just sold his house to a mortgage company and had recently become a father.

Zorka demonstrates his little iron man for Monk in *The Phantom Creeps*.

For *Son of Frankenstein*, Lugosi was given a take-it-or-leave-it salary of $500 a week, with a contract for only one week. Producer-director Rowland V. Lee could scarcely do anything about the pinchpenny salary, but he kept Lugosi at work throughout the shooting, from November 7, 1938 through January 4, 1939. A rush job in the editing booth enabled a January 13, 1939 release.

And 1939 proved a fine, busy year for Bela Lugosi. Following *Son of Frankenstein*, he handled a small but showy role *Ninotchka* at MGM. He worked at 20th Century-Fox in *The Gorilla*; at RKO in *The Saint's Double Trouble*; and even at Disney, as an early-in-the-game model for the demon in *Fantasia*. Lugosi traveled to England to star in *Dark Eyes of London* (aka *The Human Monster*), a gruesome melodrama that curiously escaped banishment by the English censors. Lugosi signed an-

Ann Zorka (Dora Clement), the love of Alex Zorka's life, is the one thing that keeps the scientist (Bela Lugosi) calm and reasonably sane.

other multi-picture contract with Universal; his next for Universal would be *The Phantom Creeps*.

The *Hollywood Reporter* announced on January 3, 1938, a forthcoming Universal serial called *The Shadow Creeps*. No cast was mentioned. At length, the title was transformed to *The Phantom Creeps*. The finished product finds Lugosi relishing his mad-scientist role. The personality of Dr. Alex Zorka is perhaps the most generously humanized of Lugosi's villainous doctors, and it stands as an explicit blueprint for the renegade surgeon characters he would generally play for the rest of his life.

Lugosi biographer Arthur Lennig has argued persuasively that *The Invisible Ray* (1936) would have been a stronger film if Karloff and Lugosi had swapped roles. Lennig holds that the main character, rendered paranoid by radiation poisoning, seems better suited to Lugosi. Clearly, the

Creeps company had the advantage of ready reference to *The Invisible Ray*, which of course is a source of stock footage for the serial. Scenarist Willis Cooper can only have studied *The Invisible Ray* very closely when writing the basis for *The Phantom Creeps*, considering that Cooper's original script for *Son of Frankenstein* is brimming with references to Universal's two earlier *Frankenstein* films.

In *The Invisible Ray*, Karloff's Dr. Janos Rukh has found an element called Radium X, which has the power to heal or destroy. Lugosi's Dr. Alex Zorka in *Creeps* has done likewise. Both Rukh and Zorka are scorned by the scientific establishment, and both live in seclusion.

In his madness, Rukh feels that his collaborators have stolen his discovery. Zorka, betrayed, finds that at one time or another his discovery (the chunk of meteorite) has been stolen by foreign and/or domestic agents. In one of his last purely kind acts, Rukh forces his wife out of his life, lest she be killed or contaminated. Similarly, Zorka's wife (Dora Clement) is accidentally killed in a plane crash that Zorka believes was caused by the federal government; he swears vengeance. Both Rukh and Zorka fake their deaths so that they can carry on with their outlaw research. In *Ray*, Rukh's former ally, Dr. Felix Benet (Lugosi, underplaying beautifully), decides that he must stop Rukh at all costs. In *Creeps*, former colleague Fred Mallory (Edwin Stanley) feels he must thwart Zorka. A key difference is that Benet feels only compassion for Rukh, where Mallory treats Zorka with an icy detachment and no trace of abiding loyalty.

Zorka has become an outcast in the scientific community as a consequence of his controversial experiments, which involve a powerful element from a meteorite unearthed in Africa. Mallory feels that Zorka is working "contrary to the good of mankind." Zorka's wife is the only person who can communicate with the embittered scientist. Even at the character's most extreme lengths of misconduct, Lugosi conveys the spirit of a good man gone wrong.

The death of Zorka's wife kills off any goodness remaining. His festering resentments finally consume him. Zorka becomes ever more furious as he finds himself in the midst of government agents and foreign spies trying to take his great source of power. This plot of a mad search for a deadly mystery box would become the basis for a seminal film noir, *Kiss Me Deadly* (1955), based on a novel by Mickey Spillaine and directed by Robert Aldrich.

THE New UNIVERSAL presents

BELA LUGOSI
in

THE **PHANTOM CREEPS**

with
Robert KENT · Dorothy ARNOLD
Regis TOOMEY · Edward Van SLOAN

12 SPINE-SHIVERING ACTION CHAPTERS!

Dr. Zorka expects—even demands—the worst of every situation, and he gets it. His zeal plants in the viewer a forbidden sympathy that actually makes the government's forces of order seem the villains of the piece. If Lugosi has been forced into becoming the bad guy, he aims to convert the audience to his point of view.

Apparently scripters from Republic Pictures were impressed with Lugosi's hot-blooded mad scientist. The studio released *Mysterious Doctor Satan* in 1940, which included an evil scientist named Dr. Satan who, like Zorka, has a robot and several deadly inventions, although Dr. Satan (Eduardo Cianelli) is as cold-blooded as Zorka was hot-blooded.

Directors Ford Beebe and Saul A. Goodkind mix an unusual depth of character into the requisite action, even to the awkward point of compromising the pace. Ford Beebe, Jr. has spoken revealingly of his father's methods:

> He worked at home on almost all of his preparation, including his writing, and I'm sure you know that he wrote [without for-

Dr. Alex Zorka (Lugosi) admires his nasty looking robot, much to the dismay of his assistant Monk (Jack C. Smith) in *The Phantom Creeps*.

mal recognition] more than half of the films that he directed later, so that his preparation was a big part of the result... And he wrote his whole script, and I don't mean the plot, I mean he wrote the scene cuts—the dialogue, everything—mentally, before he sat down at the typewriter, and then he wrote the whole thing! He'd stop to sleep a little in the daytime, and he was a fast typist! He could type 100 words [a minute] if he wanted to, and he could type fast! I can just hear that machine going! And that's what he did! That's the way he prepared for the production.

Lugosi, saddled with the imperative to create a larger-than-life villain for the benefit of a chiefly juvenile audience, nonetheless brings to

Monk has ruined another Zorka scheme in *The Phantom Creeps*. (Photofest)

the role a wealth of emotional nuances and a gradual sense of deterioration. When Zorka accidentally causes a train wreck, he shows a remorse wholly unexpected in his scheme of vengeance.

By comparison with what Republic Pictures was doing by now in the serial realm, *The Phantom Creeps* is almost nonstop talk. Even Lugosi's magnificently absurd robot, a scowling creation that looks as laughable as it looks scary, has little to do but pose a recurring implied threat.

The supporting players are adequate or better. Robert Kent brings more than is written to the key heroic role. Conversely, Dorothy Arnold brings less than is written to her portrayal of a spunky journalist. Dora Clement is most believable in the small but pivotal role of Ann Zorka.

Uniformly good are Regis Toomey as a government man, Jack C. Smith as Zorka's disloyal and harebrained assistant and *Dracula*'s Edward Van Sloan as the chief spy.

The serial's real drawback lies in its editing. Ford Beebe, Jr. states that often sloppy editing was due to Ben Pivar's intervention. Pivar, who would later produce low-budget horror films for the studio, was related to Maurice Pivar, the head of Universal's editing department. Beebe, Jr. noted:

> ...This guy knew nothing about cutting. But he would be going around to all the cutting rooms and he had a lot of studio clout... about who was going to do what and the proper way to do it. Frankly he didn't know [anything]. They wouldn't turn it directly over to a good editor. It [the studio] had all this supervision by people who weren't as competent as the actual editors themselves. This actually happened in a lot of features, too.

The pacing is slow to the point of plodding, and the sloppy manner in which mismatched shots are strung together presents a real problem with continuity and aesthetic sense. The most infuriating mismatch is the sequence where Zorka bombs an airship, with a segué to documentary footage of the *Hindenburg* disaster of 1937—which was still fresh in the minds of moviegoers in 1939. Republic, too, had used *Hindenburg* footage—even earlier, in *Dick Tracy Returns* (1938).

Ford Beebe, Jr. told me about the problems of serial continuity:

> [W]hen you don't shoot consecutive scenes in the same order..., you have to maintain a tremendous amount of that in your mind... [Characters] could get wounded or something. Then, you'd shoot something that was done before they were hurt, and then something after. In projects [where characters are] smoking, to watch

the cigarettes alone was almost a one-person job. A guy doesn't come in on one scene with a cigarette that's almost a butt, and then in the following close-up, have a new cigarette smoking!

They [the editing department] would go ahead and make a first cut on their own, but they really didn't have the time or the money to go back and do it over, because most of those things had release dates on them before they were finished. If something was done real poorly, yes, he [Ford Beebe, Sr.] got a chance to see it, but he didn't get a chance to see it a reel at a time, or go in and look over the editor's shoulder, or anything like that. I doubt that he would have had a final say, either, but I know that he had an opportunity—it was more, though, when the editor was in a pickle then when it was already done. An editor might say, "Gee, I don't see how I can get this working right!" and my Dad would go and see if he could help him out.

Like *The Return of Chandu*—flaws in either case notwithstanding—*The Phantom Creeps* is a wonderful showcase for Lugosi. From a historical viewpoint, *Creeps* may seem a demotion for the star, given that the actor's fellow players from *Son of Frankenstein*, Basil Rathbone and Boris Karloff, were appearing in Universal's prestigious production of *Tower of London* around this time. Be that as it may, *The Phantom Creeps* was given an unusually high promotional profile: It was generously publicized, in both the tradepapers and the popular press, and was even adapted into a comic book, one of the first motion pictures to be granted that mass-media distinction. Lugosi seems to be enjoying himself in what would be not only his final serial, but also his last chance to carry a Universal picture.

Co-director Ford Beebe had been involved with serials since the silent days. Beebe handled much of the second-unit work on *Son of Fran-*

Dr. Zorka and his shifty assistant Monk check out the listening devices in *The Phantom Creeps***. (Photofest)**

kenstein, supplementing the efforts of assistant director Fred Frank, and Beebe was probably more aware of Bela Lugosi's range and abilities than most other directors on the Universal lot. Beebe at one point drafted a proposed screenplay called *Dracula vs. the Wolf Man*, with Lugosi's portrayal of Count Dracula clearly in mind; this project was reworked by other hands into the matched set of *House of Frankenstein* and *House of Dracula* in 1944-45.

Ford Beebe, Sr. once told historian Richard Bojarski of the advantages of working with Lugosi:

> Because retakes were minimal..., [h]e worried about forgetting his lines. As a precaution, he had his lines written on

scraps of paper, most of which were hidden out of camera range, in his pockets, and other parts of his clothing. But this was typical of Bela, who was a fine, hard-working perfectionist.

The precautions make sense: Lugosi had a tremendous amount of dialogue to remember and deliver in a short time. Among Universal's production documents, housed at the University of Southern California, there is a running account showing that *The Phantom Creeps* was assigned a budget of $133,100.00 (including 30 percent studio overhead). Week-by-week status reports follow herewith:

- "…We are experiencing a little difficulty with Lugosi on dialogue and also with the many trick gags necessary for a subject of this type. However, it appears quite possible at this time that we will be able to finish up right on schedule May 24 and very close to approved budget."
- "Although this serial is encountering some difficulty on exterior work due to foggy conditions every morning, they are maintaining schedule, and if we meet up with no illness or other unforeseen delays, we should finish up right on schedule .."
- "This serial has been moving along very consistently during the past week and have been working a few nights in an effort to finish up on Tuesday, May 23, one day under their 24-day schedule." (The serial wrapped principal photography on Thursday, May 25, 1939, for a total of 25 days, one day behind the original schedule.)
- "The miniature work on this serial has finished up this morning [June 10,

1939], and the editing should be sufficiently advanced to record our musical score some time next week." (The musical score was recorded on June 17. Final cost was calculated at $132,000 on a basis of 25 percent studio overhead.)

With the budget and time constraints, it is a wonder that the serial turned out so well. Although it must have seemed otherwise to Beebe, the head office patently was aware of his talents, and at length Beebe was promoted to feature-film projects, including the almost uniformly excellent *Night Monster* (1942). *Night Monster* is said to have impressed visiting director Alfred Hitchcock, who professed astonishment that Beebe had delivered the film so rapidly and in such polished form.

Despite its pacing and inescapably cheap texture, *The Phantom Creeps* is an enjoyable serial. There is a fascinating array of footage from such finer sources as *The Invisible Man* (1933), *The Invisible Ray* (1936), *Frankenstein* (1931) and *Son of Frankenstein* (1939). The *Frankenstein* series clips were needed because Universal did not own the machines or the services of electrical genius Kenneth Strickfaden, who had created the distinctive look of the *Frankenstein* laboratory. The weird machinery that should have been crackling away in Dr. Zorka's laboratory was now in service at Republic Pictures.

Dorothy Arnold, Bela Lugosi and the robot on the cover of *Movie Comics*, **No. 6.**
(Courtesy of Ronald V. Borst/Hollywood Movie Posters)

A strike by musicians had by now forced the industry to make new soundtrack recordings rather than indulge in its old-standby tactic of using stock musical tracks. This situation explains why some of the familiar pieces from Franz Waxman's score for *Bride of Frankenstein*, Karl Hajos' score for *Werewolf of London*, Clifford Vaughan's score for *The*

Raven (all 1935) and Frank Skinner's score for *Son of Frankenstein* (1939) sound somehow different when encountered in *The Phantom Creeps*.

The serial-makers not only recycled music and footage, they also recycled plots. Clearly, there are elements from *The Invisible Man* and *The Invisible Ray* in the narrative continuity of *The Phantom Creeps*. But *Creeps*, in its turn, also proved influential: Practically all of Lugosi's resentful psychologists, chemists, atomic scientists and brain surgeons from *The Devil Bat* to *Bride of the Monster* owe a debt to the defining attitude of this grand-manner mad scientist in *The Phantom Creeps*. The title remains a fine conversation piece, too—even among those souls who wouldn't be caught dead watching a serial. Writer and historian Michael Price feels, "most people find the title amusing on first blush because they take the word *Creeps* as a verb, rather than a noun."

The influential tradepaper, *Variety*, weighed in on a favorable note: "Universal's latest chapter play gains considerable box-office lift from the presence of Bela Lugosi, arch-villain of horror features... [He] develops his characterization convincingly, even in the more implausible situations."

The *Motion Picture Herald* characterized *The Phantom Creeps* as being "on the fantastic side"—okay, and so what else is new?—adding: "But is an absorbing work."

If one were pressed to choose only a couple of these serials as essential viewing for the Lugosi fan, *The Return of Chandu* (1934) would have to be on the list. Lugosi's portrayal is probably the closest thing we have to help us envision him as the romantic leading man he had been on the stage.

From a technical standpoint, *SOS Coast Guard* (1937) is superb. The pacing, editing, plot, musical scoring and special effects—considering the budget—are exceptional. It is everything technically that one might wish of *The Phantom Creeps*. However, there just isn't enough of Lugosi.

On the other hand, Lugosi's zestful performance in *The Phantom Creeps* (1939) is what keeps the serial enjoyable despite its slowed pace and clunky editing. Lugosi seems to have enjoyed making these serials—especially *Creeps*—and as always, he took his job as seriously as if he were playing to a more discriminating audience.

We might characterize Lugosi as a Don Quixote among Hollywood stars—a player determined to make something special out of the increasingly cheap movies he found himself making as the years dragged on. In

Zorka is about to perform "painless surgery" on Monk in *The Phantom Creeps*.

the final resolve, Bela Lugosi was—to borrow a line from writer Bob Madison—"a large spirit in a town with a small soul."

CREDITS: Associate Producer: Henry MacRae; Directors: Ford Beebe and Saul A. Goodkind; Story: Willis Cooper; Screenplay: George Plympton, Basil Dickey and Mildred Barish; Dialogue Director: Lyonel Margolis; Camera: Jerry Ash and William Sickner; Art Direction: Ralph M. DeLacey; Edited by Alvin Todd, Irving Birnbaum and Joseph Glick; a Serial in 12 Chapters; Feature-Length Version, 75 Minutes, in Later Distribution by: Commonwealth Pictures; Released: July 27, 1939

CAST: Bela Lugosi (Dr. Alex Zorka), Robert Kent (Captain Bob West), Regis Toomey (Jim Daly), Dorothy Arnold (Jean Drew), Edward Van Sloan (Chief Jarvis), Eddie Acuff (Mac), Anthony Averill (Rankin), Edwin Stanley (Dr. Mallory), Jack C. Smith (Monk), Roy Barcroft (Parker), Forrest Taylor (Black), Karl Hackett (Brown), Robert Blair (Smith), Jerry Frank (Jones), Dora Clement (Ann Zorka), Hugh Huntley (Perkins),

Artwork from the comic book version o*f The Phantom Creeps* (1939). (Courtesy of Ronald V. Borst/Hollywood Movie Posters)

Charles King (Buck), Edward Wolff or "Bud" Wolff (Robot), Lee J. Cobb (Construction Worker)

CHAPTER TITLES: 1) "The Menacing Power"; 2) "Death Stalks the Highways"; 3) "Crashing Towers"; 4) "Invisible Terror"; 5) "Thundering Rails"; 6) "The Iron Monster"; 7) "The Menacing Mist"; 8) "Trapped in the Flames"; 9) "Speeding Doom"; 10) "Phantom Footprints"; 11) "The Blast"; 12) "To Destroy the World"

Sinister Serials: Lon Chaney, Jr.

CHAPTER FIVE
Like Father, Like Son:
The Sinister Serials of
Lon Chaney, Jr.

While Bela Lugosi pulled out all the stops as the maniacal Dr. Alex Zorka in *The Phantom Creeps*, a new horror star was quietly rising—Lon Chaney, Jr. (1906-1973). Boris Karloff was busy making films at Columbia and Monogram, and with a fresh contract at Universal the Englishman posed renewed competition for Lugosi, even though *Son of Frankenstein* (1939) proved the richest representation yet of their collaborative presence. Neither Karloff nor Lugosi had experienced an easy climb to fame: Both toiled far longer than the younger Chaney, on screen and on the legitimate stage, before achieving popular acclaim. All the same, the son of Lon Chaney, the silent screen's most driven actor, had an exceptionally tough go of paying his dues. Years of modest roles, punctuated by the occasional starring assignment on Hollywood's Poverty Row, can be blamed as much upon an ill-managed career as upon Junior's unabashed taste for strong drink.

Early on, he had preferred to work under his christened name, Creighton Chaney. By the middle 1930s, the industry convinced him—under duress, he often complained—to take up the Lon, Jr. identity. The overdue breakthrough came with Hal Roach's production of *Of Mice and Men* (1939), in the role of a childlike giant who cannot control his own strength.

The portrayal caused the industry to take notice, and Universal Pictures offered Chaney a contract. *Man Made Monster* (1941) became Junior's first horror film at the preeminent horror studio—a retooling of an undeveloped story property, once intended for Karloff and Lugosi, called *The Electric Man*. The modest production became a hit, establishing the young artist as Universal's new star in a revitalized genre. (This was hardly the first time a script planned for Karloff and/or Lugosi would go to other talents: The 1935 *WereWolf of London* had been envisioned as a title-role vehicle for Karloff, with Lugosi as a secondary creature. Instead, it featured Henry Hull and Warner Oland in the respective roles.)

While *Man Made Monster* was taking shape, a new script was being readied with Lugosi in mind for a werewolf role. It would prove to be a worthwhile turn for Lugosi, all right—but a supporting part. The film would turn out to be *The Wolf Man* (1941), and the star role of the doomed Larry Talbot would fall to Lon Chaney, Jr.

Strange, how the cosmic dots connect, one to the other. Bela Lugosi once was considered the successor to the elder Lon Chaney, with the touchstone of the leading role in *Dracula* (1931). With *The Wolf Man*, Chaney, Jr. became the successor not only to Lugosi but to Karloff, as well.

Creighton Tull Chaney was born on February 10, 1906. A careworn childhood—to use a word that Junior himself often would invoke—found him constantly on the road with his parents, Lon and Cleva Chaney, on the town-to-town Vaudeville circuit. By the time that Lon had successfully anchored his career, Creighton was already a teenager. Long estrangements, brought on by his mother's emotional instability and alcoholism, culminated in divorce. During these periods, Creighton lived with his father. Lon, the elder, was so embittered by the split that he told his son that Cleva had died. Many years passed before Creighton learned the truth. His father had discouraged the boy's fascination with show business and the moviemaking racket. By the late 1920s, Creighton had gone to work for General Water Heater Corp. in California. When Lon Chaney died in 1930, Creighton found himself pondering a future in pictures.

"Dad was dead-set against my having *anything* to do with the business," Junior told the film journalists George E. Turner and Michael H. Price in 1969.

> I always thought picture-making looked
> like *some fun*—and Dad always impressed
> upon me the rigors and the sacrifices of
> the game. Dad was one intense cuss, and I
> respected his wishes, even against my own.
> Then, his death got me to thinkin' more

Mary Philbin and Lon Chaney, Sr. in *Phantom of the Opera* (1925).

and more about the pictures, and my drinkin' buddies encouraged me to give it a go. Some fun—*hah*! It turned out to be as rigorous and demeaning as he'd described it, but always with its rewards. Always with its rewards.

Turner described Junior as "outgoing and expressive, especially when in the company of folks who didn't put on airs." Other accounts, from the 1940s, find him to have been considered withdrawn and hardly the type to circulate among Hollywood's elite. Turner said:

Lon Chaney, Jr. in his breakthrough performance in *Of Mice and Men*.

Junior was no schmoozer but he loved to hang out with the blue-collar rank-and-file, the Teamsters and stagehands and plain ol' working-class guys in general. He was constantly being upbraided, he told me, by the little big shots at Universal for playing poker backstage with the grips when he was supposed to be on set.

Glenn Strange, the character actor who eventually would inherit the role of Universal's Frankenstein Monster, recalled Junior in similarly fond terms:

Just a pair of easygoin' roughnecks, that's all we were—nothin' in common with the upper crust, but plenty in common with one another. I paid a kind of a backhanded tribute to Lonnie in that little imitation wolf-man picture I made called *The Mad Monster* [1943], playin' the human personality as a sort of *Mice and Men* lamebrain, and then of course doin' the creature as a takeoff on *The Wolf Man*. Lonnie never *would* let me live that down! He'd rib me about knockin' off two of his pictures at once, for years to come!

Chaney and fellow actor Russell Wade were friends from way back, owing to Junior's marriage to Patsy Beck, sister of Wade's childhood pal, Bob Beck. Mrs. Russell Wade gave me a different look at Chaney, Jr.:

I thought his personality was rather drab, but I wasn't that familiar with him... He wasn't warm, and you didn't get to know him real fast... I'm quite sure he was a very nice human being, but I never got to know him really well.

Chaney biographer Don G. Smith hints persuasively that Chaney harbored a distrust of women as a consequence of his experiences with his mother. Ford Beebe, Jr., son of the great serial director, takes a broader view, ascribing the distance that Chaney kept from other people—at least on tentative acquaintance—to an inability to shake the influence of his famous father.

I think, like a lot of second-generation picture people, that he had a little trouble getting away from his father's image, and a lot of people did that....It's a psychological thing. They don't want to get a reputation for being like their parents; they want to be their own actor—or whatever their field is—and it presents a problem.

Creighton Chaney had made up his mind within a year of his father's death: He wanted to become an actor. RKO-Radio Pictures was first to put the youngster to work, and after a few bit parts he proved himself ready to carry a production. (Mascot's Red Grange serial, *The Galloping Ghost* [1931] has been mistakenly cited as containing a small performance by Chaney.) The breakthrough was RKO's serialized remake of Cecil B. DeMille's *The Last Frontier* (1928)—a strategic choice, inasmuch as the silent original would supply much spectacular footage. The new version would be an efficient way to test the worth of the son of the great Lon Chaney.

THE LAST FRONTIER
(RKO-Radio; 1932)

"I remember him as being a big man," the daughter of director Spencer Gordon Bennet told me in recalling Creighton Chaney, "but then, *everyone* looked big to me at that time."

As a privileged visitor to her father's closed shooting sets as a child, Harriet Bennet Pessis would grow up to harbor invaluable memories of the making of *The Last Frontier*. "We used to ride the motion picture horses," Mrs. Pessis said.

> I remember Mary Jo Desmond was in [the serial]. She was William Desmond's granddaughter. When she wasn't working, we'd go off and ride... [A]t Kernville..., they had a Western town set built up there, [and] all the [motion picture] companies used to go up there if they needed a Western set. Later on, they made a big dam out on the Kern River, and they flooded the whole little town... It's no longer there.

The serial begins to the strains of a traditional cowboy ballad, "The Old Chisholm Trail," and we learn early on that the spring of 1876 saw "the fiercest Indian fighting in the history of the West." In Morrisonville, benevolent and beloved patriarch Lige Morris (played by Richard Neil) leads a malicious secret life as the brains behind a gun-running racket, selling stolen military weapons to renegade Indians.

Creighton Chaney plays Tom Kirby, crusading publisher of Morrisonville's *Weekly Monitor*. Tom has an adopted daughter, Aggie, who had been rescued from an Indian uprising. Tom's friend, Happy (Slim Cole), a bearded bear of a man, is like an uncle to Tom and the girl. Tom is in love with Betty Halliday (Dorothy Gulliver), daughter of Army Colonel Halliday (Claude Payton). Colonel Halliday is besieged by attacks and sabotage, which continue despite the assurances of General Custer (William Desmond) that things will get better.

Tom Kirby suspects Lige Morris right away, but Morris enjoys a sterling reputation. Unfortunately, there is not much of a confrontation between the good and the evil here, because Richard Neil's villainy is so one-dimensional. He sneers and rubs his hands together with glee as if the serial had been made in 1912 and not 1932. Now, this overcooked performance would not be bad if Neil had thrown in a little color, as Charles Middleton or Noah Beery, Sr. might have done. Even when Neil half-heartedly pretends to be sympathetic, there is nothing in his performance that makes you want to despise him the way that Henry Brandon or Boris Karloff or Bela Lugosi could do when they got a juicy, villainous role they could sink their teeth into. Because there seems to be corruption everywhere, Tom Kirby disguises himself as a Zorro-like character called the Black Ghost, affecting an exaggerated Spanish accent. Either as himself or the Black Ghost, Kirby finds plenty of excitement and danger as he rescues Betty Halliday and other friends from the forces of antisocial misconduct.

Morris has been blackmailing Jeff Maitland (Francis X. Bushman, Jr.) and his wife, Rose (Judith Barrie), who must pretend to be Maitland's sister for hidden reasons. Rose suspects that her husband is involved with sabotage. Jeff redeems himself at the end of the story, almost at the cost of his own life. Through his own courage and that of his friends, Tom Kirby is able to break up the racket, stop the uprisings and win the love of Betty Halliday.

Pathé was no longer making serials at this time, and so producer Amadée J. Van Beuren released the serial through RKO's short-subjects division. The production was mounted independently. Associate producer Fred J. McConnell had to borrow Creighton Chaney, in effect, from RKO, even though the studio was committed from the start to distribute the serial. McConnell had been involved with producing serials at Universal. The Van Beuren Corp. released its own short subjects, including retooled-for-sound versions of Charlie Chaplin's comedies, but produced numerous primitive animated cartoons for RKO release.

George Plympton and Robert Hill were veteran serial writers by then, and why they—even with Spencer Bennet's help—failed to come up with a more exciting yarn is anyone's guess. In terms of plot and thrills, *Frontier* pales by comparison with any top-of-the-line serial of the period, but is certainly no worse than the typical serial from Mascot Pictures. Most early talkies—whether serial, short subject or feature-

lengther—suffer from slow pacing, a consequence of the industry's sluggish adjustment to the need to reconcile sight with sound.

Creighton Chaney tries his best to carry the serial. Dorothy Gulliver, a favorite actress at Mascot, is impressive as the romantic interest. Francis X. Bushman, Jr. as the fallen hero Jeff Maitland, is fine. He and Creighton Chaney had a great deal of family baggage in common, for Bushman's father, Francis X. Bushman, had been a major star of the silent era. Several years later, Lon Chaney, Jr. would go out of his way to help the elder Bushman regain recognition within the industry. Judith Barrie does a more than adequate job as Rose Maitland. William Desmond is a bit too hammy as General Custer, but it is important to remember that the serial was made years before Errol Flynn gave the character a more dashing image. Desmond's granddaughter, Mary Jo, is bright and resilient as Tom Kirby's daughter. Slim Cole, as the good-hearted Happy, is unforgettable.

Chaney once told historian Calvin T. Beck about the rigors of the serial:

Tom Kirby (Lon Chaney, Jr.) is attacked by Lige Morris' gang in *The Last Frontier*.

> I'd never really ridden a horse... And the
> first thing they had me do was get 20 feet
> up in a tree and leap on a villain as he gal-
> loped by beneath me... We did a hundred
> scenes a day.

Chaney's reminiscence is reflected and amplified in an article by
Nancy Pryor in the January 1933 issue of *Movie Classic* magazine:

> Chaney was called upon to leap from a tree
> onto the back of a supposed-to-be runaway
> horse. He is only a passable horseman, but

the son of Lon did that perilous stunt—
and dislocated his hip, fractured a thumb
and broke a rib! To many who worked on
the picture with him, this will be the first
news they have of the injury the boy did
himself. Creighton didn't mention it—he
didn't even ask for the services of a doctor.

In another chapter... Creighton, who is
only a fair swimmer, leaped into some
charging rapids and performed a swim-
ming stunt that would have been difficult
for Johnny Weissmuller—at the cost of a
dislocated shoulder!

It is a leap of faith to trust the movie-fan magazines, but the Pryor
article has an uncommon ring of truth and immediacy. Chaney obviously worked hard on *The Last Frontier*, but he was better prepared to
accept the rigors of the assignment than he was to carry a leading role.
Had Chaney possessed the advantage of experience, the picture might
compare favorably with a superior serial like Buck Jones' star vehicle,
Gordon of Ghost City, made just a year later at Universal.

Director Spencer Gordon Bennet worked closely with the writers,
said Harriet Pessis:

He used to give them ideas. More than a
story line, just an idea how to do something. He used to make trick shots because
he didn't have the special effects [in the
budget]. He always liked to sit in on the
story conferences. He usually had a couple
of weeks before the serial or feature would
start. I can always remember him sitting
in with the writers.

He just always gave his best on what
he was doing. He just was that type of person... My Dad would stay up [working]
for hours! Oh, he had tremendous energy,

he never sat down! If he did sit down, he was asleep! I can always remember my Dad when he was on a picture, staying up late at night, working over his scripts, then getting up early to go on location. It was very, very traumatic for him when he did do a movie. You know, he put his whole heart and soul into it. Everything!

He almost had a stock company. He always used to like to get the same stuntmen. He and Yakima Canutt were quite friendly. Yak used to work in a lot of his movies, and then, of course, he became quite well known. He used to visit the house. I'm looking over his [Bennet's] credits, here, and I see the same names all the time. They knew that if Dad had a part for them—anything—he would hire them. But then, he had to get actors that knew what they were doing, because he worked so fast!

He did cut the film in the camera, because he had once been an editor. In fact [in the early days], he edited his own films... A lot of editors became directors.

The matching of Bennet's footage with scenes taken from the 1928 DeMille version is hardly seamless. The older sequences have a speeded-up look, characteristic of silent footage projected at the higher sound-film rate of 24 frames per second. Some of the action is terrific—shot from a mobile camera's point of view during horseback chases, or tracking a wagon thundering out of control. The long shots of a buffalo stampede lend an epic grandeur.

Compromising the serial's relevance to the present day is an abundance of ethnic humor, with a black character serving as the butt of an extended gag about ghosts. It is a cheap laugh, and an easy scene for writers to construct, relying on stock stereotyped characters that go back to Vaudeville and the yet earlier minstrel tradition.

Dorothy Gulliver comforts Lon Chaney, Jr. in *The Last Frontier*. (Photofest)

Finally, near the end of the last chapter, the bad guys are subdued and Lige Morris' scheming character has been done in by a stampede. All is peaceful, but Tom Kirby puts on his Black Ghost disguise once again—for playful purposes. He snuggles up to Betty Halliday and awaits a declaration from her.

"You have been my great friend," she says, "and I like you very much! But I love someone else!"

"And this man that you love, is it Señor Kirby? No? Yes?" asks the Black Ghost. Betty nods. The Ghost continues: "Oh, that is so sad! He is not worthy of such as you! You're sweet! So lovely! I hear this Señor Kirby has loved many ladies, is it not so?"

"No doubt he has loved many ladies," she replies, "but he loves me, and always will!"

"I have declared my love for you!" the Ghost says "Has this Señor Kirby done so much, like I have?"

"No!" she snaps back. "But I love him, and I feel Tom really loves me!"

Here Kirby drops the Ghost act, resuming his natural voice, "What makes you think Tom Kirby loves you?" He sheds the Ghost disguise.

"Tom Kirby!" shouts Betty. "I'll never speak to you again! Coaxing a confession out of me, then laughing at my love!"

He laughs, "But honey, I was only teasin'!" and leans forward to kiss her.

Betty, not quite as angry as she was a moment ago, chides him, "Tom Kirby, don't you dare!" Naturally, they embrace.

The scene almost works, closing the adventure on a note of unadulterated mush that can only have sent a majority of the film's adolescent male audience stampeding for the lobby. Dorothy Gulliver is perfectly capable here, but Chaney is clearly unsure of himself as an actor.

Chaney biographer Don G. Smith characterizes the lead acting as "a very wooden performance. As the Ghost, [Chaney's] attempt at a Spanish accent is particularly laughable... *The Last Frontier* laid bare Chaney's weaknesses as an actor. While physically promising, he was not a natural in any sense of the word."

On August 13, 1932, *Billboard* magazine offered this tantalizing announcement: "Universal starts work on the new serial, *The Lost Special*, with Creighton Chaney, Cecilia Parker and Caryl Lincoln in the leads." It didn't happen, after all—at least, not with Chaney—but even the distant "what if?" prospect of Junior's arriving so prematurely at Universal suggests what might have led to a fascinating connection with Boris Karloff and Bela Lugosi. But no, the Conan Doyle-derived railroad mystery *The Lost Special* wound up instead starring Frank Albertson, along with Ernie Nevers, Cecilia Parker and Caryl Lincoln.

CREDITS: Associate Producer: Fred J. McConnell; Directors: Spencer Gordon Bennet and Thomas L. Storey; Original Story: Courtney Ryley Cooper; Dialogue and Continuity: George Plympton and Robert F. Hill; Photographed by: Edward Snyder and Gilbert Warrington; Art Director: E.E. Sheeley; Film Editor: Thomas Malloy; Sound: RCA Recording; a Serial in 12 Chapters; Feature Version, *The Black Ghost*, Running Time: 65 Minutes; Released: September 5, 1932

CAST: Creighton Chaney (Tom Kirby/"The Black Ghost"); Dorothy Gulliver (Betty Halliday); Mary Jo Desmond (Aggie Kirby); Francis X. Bushman, Jr. (Jeff Maitland); Joe Bonomo (Blackie); Slim Cole (Happy); Judith Barrie (Rose Maitland); Richard Neil [given elsewhere as "Neal" and "Neill"] (Lige Morris); William Desmond (General Custer); LeRoy Mason (Buck); Yakima Canutt (Wild Bill Hickok); Pete Morrison (Hank); Claude Payton (Colonel Halliday); Fritzi Fern (Maria Morris); Bill Nestell (Tex); and Benny Corbett, Fred Burns, Leo Cooper, Frank Lackteen, Walt Robbins, Ray Steel

CHAPTER TITLES: 1) "The Black Ghost Rides"; 2) "The Thundering Herd"; 3) "The Black Ghost Strikes"; 4) "Fatal Shot"; 5) "Clutching Sands"; 6) "The Terror Trail"; 7) "Doomed"; 8) "Facing Death"; 9) "Thundering Doom"; 10) "The Life Line"; 11) "Driving Danger"; 12) "The Black Ghost's Last Ride"

THE THREE MUSKETEERS
(Mascot Pictures Corp.; 1933)

Armand Corday (Creighton Chaney), a solemn young member of the French Foreign Legion, is in trouble. While talking with his sister, Elaine (Ruth Hall), and a friend, Tom Wayne (John Wayne)—an American flyer who has volunteered his services to the Legion—Armand seems nervous and evasive. Tom believes that Armand is on a top-secret mission.

It develops, however, that Armand has been forced to work with a terrorist movement, headed by an elusive outlaw known as El Shaitan. Armand enters a hidden meeting place and defies a command from the ringleader, "...I've done your dirty work because I was afraid of being found out! ...I'm through with you and your infernal Devil's Circle!"

El Shaitan warns him that death is the only way out of the mob. Armand resentfully allows himself to be manipulated into accepting new orders.

Lieutenant Wayne is implicated. When Wayne realizes that Armand is involved, he refuses to endanger his friend until he can learn the nature of the threat. Armand plots a getaway, only to be interrupted by El Shaitan. Armand attempts suicide, but Wayne intervenes.

One of the Three Musketeers is attacked by El Shaitan's henchman in *The Three Musketeers*. (Photofest)

"Pull yourself together, old man!" barks Wayne. "You shouldn't have done this!"

"What else could I do?" pleads Armand. "I betrayed my country, betrayed you, made a mess out of everything! I couldn't escape from El Shaitan!"

"El Shaitan? Who's he? ...The head of the gun runners? Well, tell me who he is, and we'll go after him!"

"I don't know!" says Armand. "I don't even know if he's a native or a white man! He's just a name. In Arabic, it means he's the Devil!"

Soon thereafter, El Shaitan shoots Armand Corday and vanishes. Tom hears Armand's last words, "Tom! Guns! Fort Moreau—El Shaitan will come to get them!"

A treacherous servant makes it appear that Tom Wayne and his friend were quarreling, and no one believes Tom's account. A forged note brands

Tom a traitor. Seeing no other way out, Tom escapes. He allies himself with three fun-loving Legionnaires, Clancy (Jack Mulhall), Renard (Raymond Hatton) and Schmidt (Francis X. Bushman, Jr.), nicknamed the Three Musketeers after the characters of Dumas' famous novel. They adopt him as their D'Artagnan.

Creighton Chaney, in the rambunctious context of a Mascot serial, proves himself far better an actor than he had been in *The Last Frontier*. This time out, of course, the pressure was off Chaney to carry the show, and he can only have absorbed a certain feel for screen presence from the up-and-coming John Wayne.

"John Wayne—now, he was a *bona fide* movie star, I mean, compared to my pretensions about tackling the pictures," Chaney told George Turner and Michael H. Price during the 1960s.

> I held him in a kind of awe, you might say, because he had already made one big picture, *The Big Trail*, and he was a veteran of the Mascot serials, to boot, whereas I hadn't even discovered yet that I was Lon Chaney, Jr. So I imagine *Musketeers* was a bigger stretch for me than I even could have known at the time, just trying to raise myself up to the standard of being in a picture with John Wayne.

Wayne's co-star, Ruth Hall, gave this account of the shooting to *Cliffhanger* magazine:

> The physical difficulties... were many, mainly because [Mascot boss] Nat Levine wanted to shoot the serial on the Mojave Desert outside of Yuma, Arizona... I was exposed to the sun so much that... my face... became pretty badly swollen, so much so, that most of my later scenes had to be shot with my back against the camera... I didn't have a double,... plus I did my own makeup and hair. The big stu-

dios... provided people to take care of those things for you, but Mascot provided nothing.

Ford Beebe, Jr. recalled additional essentials of the production:

> [T]he location shooting..., on the sand dunes,.... was to me, really interesting, and really hard, too. It's also the first place I ever saw a glass shot done. They had this big Arab fort-like thing that was supposed to be off in the distance on the top of one of those dunes, and they put people out there and placed them. And then they put the glass with a painted building on it— like about 10 feet from the camera—and jockeyed everything around to where they put that thing up on top of that sand dune, and then had the characters moving in designated areas. And I'm a son-of-a-gun if it didn't come out like those people were moving around that fort thing there, you know, half a mile away!

Beebe, Jr. also spoke of the crucial importance of the stunt work, as headed by Yakima Canutt:

> Yak [is] the guy that started stunt work as a business, where you thought about it [how to do the stunts], and wore the proper equipment. He never wore cowboy boots because they were too hard to do stunts in. But he wore tennis shoes…, rigged to where they looked like boots, so he could do stuff like jumping from the driver's seat down on to the tongue on to the wagon… You know, you'd be a nut to start doing all that stuff in cowboy boots!

Armand Corday (Lon Chaney, Jr.) considers suicide his only option in a tense scene from *The Three Musketeers*.

Mascot had a tactic, probably borrowed from Pathé's silent-screen serials, of using various actors to pretend to be the masked villain—a cheap but certain way of throwing the viewer off-guard. Wilfred Lucas is seen in disguise and heard in some of the early chapters. Yakima Canutt

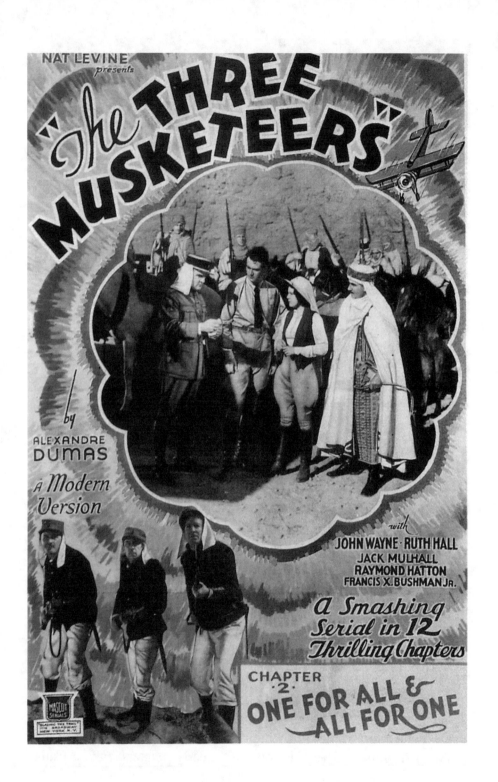

plays him in some of the episodes, and speaks a line or two as El Shaitan. Gordon De Main and Robert Frazer also portray the masked villain at one point or another.

Chaney obviously did not have the star power to carry *The Last Frontier*; however, *The Three Musketeers* shows the inklings of the good actor Chaney would one day become. John Wayne fans consider *The Three Musketeers* the best of his Mascot serials and despite typical shortcomings, *The Three Musketeers* is most enjoyable.

CREDITS: Producer: Nat Levine; Directors: Armand Schaefer and Colbert Clark; Supervising Editor: Wyndham Gittens; Story: Norman Hall, Colbert Clark, Ben Cohen and Wyndham Gittens; Dialogue: by Ella Arnold; Photographers: Ernest Miller and Tom Galligan; Music: Lee Zahler; Film Editor: Ray Snyder; Sound Engineer: Homer Ackerman; Sound: International Film Recording Co.; a Serial in 12 Chapters, 25 Reels; 1933 Feature Version: 90 Minutes; 1948 Feature Version, *Desert Command*: 70 Minutes; Released: April 7, 1933

CAST: Jack Mulhall (Clancy); Raymond Hatton (Renard); Francis X. Bushman, Jr. (Schmidt); John Wayne (Tom Wayne); Ruth Hall (Elaine Corday); Creighton Chaney (Armand Corday); Hooper Atchley (El Kadur); Gordon De Main (Colonel Duval); Robert Frazer (Major Booth); Noah Beery, Jr. (Stubbs); Al Ferguson (Ali); Edward Piel (Rankin); William Desmond (Captain Boncour); George Magrill (El Maghreb); Robert Warwick (Colonel Brent); Wilfred Lucas (El Shaitan); Merrill McCormick (Henchman); Ken Cooper (Arab); Yakima Canutt (Arab, Legionnaire, and Stunt Double)

CHAPTER TITLES: 1) "The Fiery Circle"; 2) "One for All and All for One!"; 3) "The Master Spy"; 4) "Pirates of the Desert"; 5) "Rebels' Rifles"; 6) "Death's Marathon"; 7) "Naked Steel"; 8) "The Master Strikes"; 9) "The Fatal Cave"; 10) "Trapped"; 11) "The Measure of a Man"; 12) "The Glory of Comrades"

UNDERSEA KINGDOM
(Republic Pictures Corp.; 1936)

In probably the most famous scene in this Republic trailblazer, the armored hero, Ray "Crash" Corrigan, is strapped to the front of a juggernaut, a tank-like vehicle. The arrogant and hostile Captain Hakur (Lon Chaney, Jr.) furiously demands that Corrigan surrender and help overthrow the government of Atlantis.

"All right, Corrigan, this is your last chance!" barks Chaney. "Tell your friends to hand over that blasting powder, or I'm gonna ram through the gates!"

Ray "Crash" Corrigan, Lee Van Atta and Lon Chaney, Jr. in *Undersea Kingdom*. (Photofest)

Captain Hakur (Lon Chaney, Jr.) chokes Corrigan in *Undersea Kingdom* as a mind-altered Professor Norton (C. Montague Shaw) stands by.

"Go ahead and ram!" Corrigan snaps back.

Hakur does precisely that. Corrigan, however, survives the crash—hence, no doubt, his nickname—and eventually Hakur is subdued.

This incredibly bizarre serial opens as Crash Corrigan, a football hero-turned-naval officer, agrees to accompany Professor Norton (C. Montague Shaw) on a perilous underwater mission. Professor Norton's son, Billy (Lee Van Atta), has stowed away on board. Also along for the ride are journalist Diana Compton (Lois Wilde) and Norton's assistants, the cowardly Joe (John Bradford) and the comical-but-competent Briny (Smiley Burnette) and Salty (Frankie Marvin). Norton seeks the lost city of Atlantis, which he has pegged as the source of a series of catastrophes plaguing the earth. A fantastic piece of radar-like equipment—actually, a piece of electrical effects wizard Kenneth Strickfaden's *Frankenstein* machinery—leads them to Atlantis.

This time Corrigan has got the drop on Captain Hakur and the rest of the bad guys, including the chief villain, Unga Khan (Monte Blue).

The city is inhabited by warring factions, with the good guys led by High Priest Sharad (William Farnum), and the bad guys by invading dictator Unga Khan (Monte Blue). Khan wants to conquer not only Atlantis, but also the upper world.

Like Alex Raymond's conception of the Planet Mongo in *Flash Gordon*—a bizarre blending of ancient Roman, Greek and Chinese cultures with science fiction—this version of Atlantis finds the inhabitants sporting gladiator-like apparel, with horse-drawn chariots, yet trafficking in futuristic robots, armored tanks, rockets, closed-circuit television and automated doors and elevators. Khan uses electrical gadgetry to brainwash Professor Norton into cooperating. Aligning himself with Sharad, Crash Corrigan rallies his friends to stop Khan and save Professor Norton and the surface world while they're about it.

One huge obstacle is Khan's henchman, Captain Hakur. As Hakur, Chaney enthusiastically tries every way he can to eliminate the hero. It is a performance to relish, and as true an early representation as can be found of the Junior Chaney who would finally register as a star at Universal Pictures during the early 1940s.

For all its variations on *Flash Gordon*, this serial is decisively imaginative, thanks in great measure to a brisk job of team-directing from Joseph Kane and "Breezy" Eason. The scoring is superb, with rousing musical cues from Abe Meyer's library of recordings, and most of the actors are solidly in the spirit of the yarn. It certainly is fun to see Ray Corrigan cavorting in a goofy-looking helmet and watch the exciting chariot chases as well as marvel at the special visual effects of the broth-

ers Howard and Theodore Lydecker, who, along with other technicians and artisans, worked with plenty of imagination and little money.

With *Undersea Kingdom* as only its second serial, Republic already posed serious competition for Universal's chapter-play outfit.

If there is one minor disappointment, it is in Monte Blue's indifferent portrayal of Unga Khan. Blue had started out as a snide comedian, and it's too bad he neglected to lace a bit of that mordant attitude into

his impersonation here. Where Charles Middleton brought a dimension of sardonic wit to his similarly conceived Ming the Merciless in the *Flash Gordon* serials at Universal, Blue makes Unga Khan seem merely a grump, as if suffering from a toothache.

Ray Corrigan has some of the charisma of a Buster Crabbe or a Herman Brix. Lois Wilde, as the reporter, is more decorative than (melo)dramatically interesting. Reliable C. Montague Shaw is right in his element as the tainted scientist. Kid actor Lee Van Atta is a marvel of pluck and gumption.

Lester "Smiley" Burnette and Frankie Marvin, as the comic-relief characters, are an acquired taste. At least, Burnette is less obnoxious here than in the first *Dick Tracy* serial (1937).

Chaney more than compensates, however: His Captain Hakur seems to enjoy cruelty for its own sake. The role is hardly the choicest one Chaney would tackle, but he tackles it with glee. Whether Junior's acting is memorable due to what film historians know of his subsequent work, or whether his performance has merit on its own—who can say? No one today can discover Chaney in *Undersea Kingdom* in the same way a filmgoer of 1936 could discover Chaney; there is simply too much well-known baggage in the actor's greater intervening body of work.

Republic Studio

No. Hollywood, Calif.

MUSIC CUE SHEET

Title UNDERSEA KINGDOM   Date MAY 1, 1936

Description of Picture: Serial-Episode #1   Prod. No. 417

Sound Equipment RCA VICTOR   Producer NAT LEVINE

Musical Director ABE MEYER

Reel Cue

1. Composition: LURKING	Usage: PARTIAL	
Composer: Arthur Kay-Aubran	Instrumental X	
Publisher: Southern Music Publishing	Instrumental Visual	
Rights Secured: RP Property	Vocal	Vocal Visual

2. Composition: STREAMLINE EXPRESS MAIN TITLE	Usage: PARTIAL	
Composer: Arthur Kay	Instrumental X	
Publisher: Santly Bros Joy	Instrumental Visual	
Rights Secured: RP Property	Vocal	Vocal Visual

3. Composition: AGITATO #1	Usage: PARTIAL	
Composer: Arthur Kay-Aubran	Instrumental X	
Publisher: Southern Music Publishing Co	Instrumental Visual	
Rights Secured: RP Property	Vocal	Vocal Visual

4. Composition: FERVOR	Usage: PARTIAL	
Composer: Arthur Kay	Instrumental X	
Publisher: Sam Fox Publishing Co.	Instrumental Visual	
Rights Secured: RP Property	Vocal	Vocal Visual

5. Composition: WASHINGTON POST MARCH	Usage: COMPLETE	
Composer: Sousa	Instrumental	
Publisher: Carl Fischer, Inc	Instrumental Visual X	
Rights Secured: " " "	Vocal	Vocal Visual

6. Composition: AGITATO #1	Usage: COMPLETE	
Composer: Arthur Kay-Aubran	Instrumental X	
Publisher: Southern Music Publishing Co	Instrumental Visual	
Rights Secured: RP Property	Vocal	Vocal Visual

7. Composition: LURKING	Usage: PARTIAL	
Composer: Arthur Kay-Aubran	Instrumental X	
Publisher: Southern Music Publishing Co.	Instrumental Visual	
Rights Secured: RP Property	Vocal	Vocal Visual

8. Composition: AGITATO #2	Usage: COMPLETE	
Composer: Arthur Kay-Aubran	Instrumental X	
Publisher: Southern Music Publishing Co.	Instrumental Visual	
Rights Secured: RP Property	Vocal	Vocal Visual

Music cue sheets of the scores used in *Undersea Kingdom*. (Courtesy of Lou McMahon)

Chaney biographer Don G. Smith holds that Junior "emerges as a believable physical foe for the athletic Corrigan"—which is, for that matter, all the role requires.

CREDITS: Executive Producer: Herbert J. Yates; Producer: Nat Levine; Directors: B. Reeves Eason and Joseph Kane; Supervisor: Barney Sarecky; Production Manager: Sol C. Siegel; Screenplay: John Rathmell, Maurice Geraghty and Oliver Drake; Story: Tracy Knight and John Rathmell; Supervising Editor: Joseph H. Lewis; Photographed by: William Nobles and Edgar Lyons; Process Cinematography: Ellis J. Thackery; Film Editors: Dick Fantl and Helene Turner; Sound Supervision: Terry Kellum and Harry Jones; Musical Supervision: Harry Grey; Musical Selections by: Arthur Kay, Leon Rosebrook, Meredith Willson, Reginald H. Bassett, Charles Dunworth and Joseph Carl Breil, among others; Special Effects: Jack Coyle, Ellis Thackery, and Howard and Theodore Lydecker; Art Director: E.R. Hickson [credited elsewhere to Ralph Oberg]; Wrangler: Tracy Lane; Casting: David Warner; Optical Effects: Consolidated Film Industries; Sound: RCA Victor High Fidelity Recording; a Serial in 12 Chapters, 25 Reels; 1966 Telefeature Version, *Sharad of Atlantis*, Running Time: 100 Minutes; Released: May 30, 1936

CAST: Ray "Crash" Corrigan (Crash Corrigan); Lois Wilde (Diana Compton); Monte Blue (Unga Khan); William Farnum (Sharad); Boothe Howard (Ditmar); C. Montague Shaw (Professor Norton); Lee Van Atta (Billy Norton); Lester "Smiley" Burnette (Briny Deep); Frankie Marvin (Salty); Lon Chaney, Jr. (Hakur); Lane Chandler (Darius); Jack Mulhall (Lieutenant Andrews); John Bradford (Joe); Ralph Holmes (Martos); Ernie Smith (Gourk); Lloyd Whitlock (Captain Clinton); David Horsley (Naval Sentry); Kenneth Lawton (Doctor); Raymond Hatton (Gasspon); Rube Schaffer (Magna); John Merton (Molock); Everett Kibbons (Antony); Malcolm McGregor (Zogg); Millard McGowan, William Stahl and William Yrigoyen (Chamber Guards); Jack Ingram (Man), Trace Lane (Man); and Edwin Parker, Al Seymour, George DeNormand, Alan Curtis, Tom Steele, Wes Warner, Dan Rowan

CHAPTER TITLES: 1) "Beneath the Ocean Floor"; 2) "The Undersea City"; 3) "Arena of Death"; 4) "Revenge of the Volkites"; 5) "Prisoners of Atlantis"; 6) "The Juggernaut Strikes"; 7) "The Submarine Trap"; 8) "Into the Metal Tower"; 9) "Death in the Air"; 10) "Atlantis Destroyed"; 11) "Flaming Death"; 12) "Ascent to the Upper World"

ACE DRUMMOND

(Universal Pictures Corp.; 1936)

Wrote Captain Edward V. "Eddie" Rickenbacker in his memoirs:

> I drove myself hard in those years follow-
> ing the failure of the Rickenbacker Motor
> Co., and I was all the better for it. Not only
> did the last few years of the 1920s consti-
> tute one of the happiest and most produc-

Ace Drummond (John King) and Peggy Trainor (Jean Rogers) confront Ivan (Lon Chaney, Jr.) in *Ace Drummond*.

tive periods of my life; they also served as excellent preparation for the bitter Depression of the 1930s... One venture that provided a lot of fun as well as profit was an adventure comic strip, *Ace Drummond*, based roughly on my own wartime flying experiences. I wrote the continuity myself. At the peak of *Ace*'s popularity, the strip ran in some 135 newspapers.

Rickenbacker (1890-1973) is best known as the World War I flying ace who shot down 26 enemy aircraft and battled the Red Baron, Manfred von Richthofen. When the war was over, Rickenbacker launched and lost an automobile company, then joined General Motors. Unhappy with the way GM was running Eastern Air Lines, Rickenbacker began a series of court battles to buy the airline, which he eventually took over. Resuming uniformed service during WWII, Rickenbacker crashed on a mission in the Pacific and survived with his crew members for 24 days before their rescue. His heroic fiction can only have had some basis in experience.

Rickenbacker's involvement with the *Ace Drummond* comic strip was a labor of love that proved lucrative. He developed the feature in close collaboration with the artist Clayton Knight—who had also been a World War I aviator. Rickenbacker was not a particularly gripping storyteller, and the strip's occasional surges of genuine narrative excitement suggest the helpful presence of uncredited ghost writers or script doctors from the syndicate's pool of talents. But what Rickenbacker lacked in tale-spinning moxie, he compensated for with the ring of authenticity. Knight was an exceptionally fine illustrator, and the strip was very popular. By late 1937, another artist named King Cole took over, and his looser, less true-to-life approach caused subscribing newspapers to drop *Ace Drummond* in volume.

However, the strip was a smash hit in 1936, when Universal exercised its acquisition of the movie rights. The serial concerns the problems of an airline running between the Orient and the United States—a Rickenbacker specialty. Universal had negotiated film deals for several of King Features' newspaper cartoons—also including *Secret Agent X-9*, *Jungle Jim* and *Flash Gordon*.

A suspicious-looking Ivan (Lon Chaney, Jr.), who is one of the Dragon's henchmen, from *Ace Drummond*.

Ford Beebe was back at Universal, directing serials. Beebe's son told me a great deal about the very earliest movie-business work of the master serial helmer:

> He went to Universal for the first time
> about 1914...and he was at Universal when

A young Lon Chaney, Jr. seems enchanted by Jean Rogers on the set of *Ace Drummond*. **(Photofest)**

they tried interior lighting for the first time... So a lot of the things that affected his career happened over there...

[Noticing a call posted for writers], my Dad... wrote a couple of stories, and handed them in. And one of the directors there said, "Boy! I want to use this guy! He writes the stuff so that I can take this thing and make a film out of it!"...

My Dad's career actually started at Universal, so when he came back to do the serials, he was usually hired for a longer period of time. They didn't just bring him in to do *a* serial. I kind of think *Ace Drummond* was one of the times when he just came in to do that; then he probably did some of the [writing]—developed some of it himself as they did the whole thing...

In *Ace Drummond*, Lon Chaney, Jr. plays Ivan, a henchman of a master criminal known as the Dragon. Chaney hasn't much to do other than receive and carry out orders. *Drummond* is one of the few Universal serials that resembles a Mascot serial, in that there are enough suspicious types on hand to toughen the task of spotting the real Dragon.

Junior's first scene is typical of his role. The camera pans through an array of strange-looking electrical equipment, landing on three Orientals who are hovering about a radio receiver. They have intercepted messages from an International Airlines craft, which the Dragon intends to wreck. "They've fallen into the Dragon's trap!" says Chaney. "When the pilot answers, let him have it!"

Another underling, Sergei (Stanley Blystone), activates a switch, and a pilot is electrocuted. Then a second pilot is zapped, and the plane crashes. Ace Drummond (John King), a government agent, is called in to set matters right. Drummond loves to sing as much as he loves to fly, and his tendency to belt out one groaner, "Give Me a Ship and a Song," at every opportunity becomes an annoyance in short order. Of course, the serial was made for youngsters to see at the rate of one chapter a week, not several chapters at a sitting, so modern-day viewers can spare themselves the tortures of musical overkill by watching the picture in small doses. John King, a former featured artist with bandleader Ben Bernie, has a pleasant, clean-cut personality on camera. He later found his truer niche as a singing cowboy star.

Drummond becomes interested in Peggy Trainor (Jean Rogers), who is searching for her father (C. Montague Shaw, back in harness as a scientist). Professor Trainor has disappeared during an archeological expedition. Some of the members of the expedition don't want Drummond snooping around either. Drummond has his allies, though: They include Jerry (Noah Beery, Jr.), an airplane technician; and an admiring youngster named Billy Meredith (Jackie Morrow). At a Mongolian monastery, Drummond is helped by the High Lama (Guy Bates Post). By the end of

Ace Drummond (John King) keeps an eye on a pair of diamond smugglers in *Ace Drummond*. (Photofest)

the adventure, both men are shocked to discover that the Dragon has been posing as a member of the priesthood.

Made just at the time Universal was being taken over by a cost-cutting new regime, *Ace Drummond* has that vintage Universal look and texture. John King fares okay in the leading role, but he lacks the star quality of *Flash Gordon*'s Buster Crabbe. Fans of the Three Stooges may recognize a regular Stooges foil, raspy-voiced Stanley Blystone, as one of the villains. Noah Beery, Jr., son of the great silent-movie villain Noah Beery, Sr., plays the hero's pal—the same type of role with which he would continue as late as television's *The Rockford Files*, 50 years later. Robert Warwick, James B. Leong, Sr. and Hooper Atchley all play familiar red herring parts.

Universal's stock-in-trade serial gal, Jean Rogers, has far less to do here in *Flash Gordon* and *Flash Gordon's Trip to Mars*. In an interview with *Classic Images* magazine, director Beebe recalled Miss Rogers fondly:

> I made two or three serials with Jeanie Rogers... I suspect that it was because she was so genuine that she didn't go farther in pictures. It isn't necessary for a girl to be a phony to make good in pictures, but I'm inclined to think that it helps. Jeanie was very genuine, very placid and not given to the sort of make believe la-dee-dah that attracts producers.

Russell Wade, who appears in a small role as an airline pilot, shared with me his recollections of Lon Chaney, Jr.:

> He loved to hunt and fish... [W]hen I came down here [to Indian Wells, California] to get into [the real estate] business, he gave me a briefcase. He was very nice to me! He was kind of quiet... a nice fellow... His father was a big star, I mean the biggest! And that's pretty tough for a child to come up to that! So, he felt like he hadn't made it, you know? But he was a nice guy!

Shortly after the completion of *Ace Drummond*, there were tryouts for the West Coast staging of the play *Of Mice and Men*, based on the novella by John Steinbeck. Chaney's breakthrough was practically around the corner.

Meanwhile, the theater managers who played *Ace Drummond*, week after week, registered mixed feelings about the serial. Here are some representative opinions from the picture-show industry, as quoted in the tradepaper *Motion Picture Herald*:

"This is an above-average serial as serials go," said J.E. Stocker of Detroit's Myrtle Theatre. "There is a mystery angle... that keeps them

UNIVERSAL
presents

"THE SIGN IN THE SKY"

CHAPTER number 8 of

Captain Eddie Rickenbacker's
(AMERICA'S GREATEST WAR PILOT)

"ACE DRUMMOND"

with

JOHN KING, JEAN ROGERS,
NOAH BEERY, JR, GUY BATES POST,
LON CHANEY, JR., JACKIE MORROW,
ROBERT WARWICK, ED COBB,
CHESTER GAN, JAMES LEONG

FROM THE POPULAR KING FEATURES NEWSPAPER STRIP

guessing... But why, oh why, do they do such things in serials[?] [A]s for instance at the end of Chapter 10, when the hero is seen... plunging down to pure death. At the start of Chapter 11, [there is] not the sign of a fall other than a few feet, which got the razz that it deserved. That intelligent serial producers should make such blunders is beyond me, and they do it week after week... The children look for them weekly, but even the children give those kind of endings the razz."

At the Eureka Theatre in Fabens, Texas, manager Ray Pringle reserved the right to change his mind: "This serial seems to be getting over better than average and so far has been very good." Then, over a month later, Pringle was quoted thusly in the same publication: "[T]his takes the cake for being about as dumb as any I have seen since I was a kid. It won't make me mad when this is over. The kids go for it, naturally, but I am wasting a lot of time as far as everyone else is concerned. Let's have some more as good as *Flash Gordon*."

CREDITS: Associate Producers: Barney Sarecky and Ben Koenig; Directors: Ford Beebe and Cliff Smith; Screenplay: Wyndham Gittens, Norman S. Hall and Ray Trampe; Based on the Comic Strip, *Ace Drummond*, created by Captain Eddie Rickenbacker; Photography: Richard Fryer; Supervising Editor: Saul A. Goodkind; Edited by: Edward Todd, Alvin Todd and Louis Sackin; Sound: RCA Victor; Art Direction: Ralph M. DeLacey; Main-Title Musical Scoring: Clifford Vaughan; Theme Song: "Give Me a Ship and a Song," by: Kay Kellogg; a Serial in 13 Chapters; Feature Condensation: *Squadron of Doom*; Released: September 11, 1936

CAST: John King (Ace Drummond); Jean Rogers (Peggy Trainor); Noah Beery, Jr. (Jerry); Guy Bates Post (Grand Lama); Arthur Loft (Chang-Ho); Chester Gan (Kai-Chek); Jackie Morrow (Billy Meredith); James B. Leong (Henry Kee); James Eagles (Johnny Wong); Selmer Jackson (Meredith); Robert Warwick (Winston); C. Montague Shaw (Trainor); Frederick Vogeding (Bauer); Al Bridge (Wyckoff); Lon Chaney, Jr. (Ivan); Stanley Blystone (Sergei); Ed Cobb (Nicolai); Richard Wessel (Boris); Louis Vinzinot (Lotan); Sam Ash (Le Page); Russell Wade (Airliner Pilot) and House Peters, Jr. (Co-pilot)

CHAPTER TITLES: 1) "Where East Meets West"; 2) "The Invisible Enemy"; 3) "The Doorway of Doom"; 4) "The Radio Riddle"; 5) "Bullets of Sand"; 6) "Evil Spirits"; 7) "The Trackless Trail"; 8) "The Sign in the Sky"; 9) "Secret Service"; 10) "The Mountain of Jade"; 11) "The Dragon Commands"; 12) "The Squadron of Death"; 13) "The World's Akin"

SECRET AGENT X-9
(Universal Pictures Corp.; 1937)

Secret Agent X-9 began as a newspaper comic strip drawn by Alex Raymond, already renowned as the creator of *Flash Gordon*. King Features Syndicate hired the great mystery novelist Dashiell Hammett to plot and script *X-9*, but Hammett soon lost interest in the assignment and contributed little to the finished product. King Features was just happy to have his name attached to the strip. A succession of writers and artists followed as Raymond concentrated his energies more strictly on *Flash Gordon*.

Today, this serial version of the strip is officially considered lost, although likelier its footage is merely tied up in a trademark dispute. (The American Film Institute has a print of a second *X-9* serial, which Universal produced in 1945.) The synopsis that follows relies on collector Ed Billings' transcriptions from the studio's press kit. It may be surmised that Lon Chaney, Jr., playing a henchman named Maroni, was allowed a decent amount of screen time—but the pressbook synopsis nonetheless neglects to mention Chaney or his character.

Chapter No. 1: "Modern Pirates" begins as government agents learn that a notorious jewel thief, known only as Brenda but presumably a man, is heading toward the United States. The G-Men have no likeness by which to spot Brenda. The likely quarry is a collection of foreign crown jewels, which Baron Michael Karsten (Monte Blue) has exhibited to the public. A guard is murdered, and the jewels are stolen.

Secret Agent X-9 (Scott Kolk) follows and learns that a bandit known as Blackstone (Henry Brandon) has hidden the booty in a safe deposit vault and taken the bank receipt to an art gallery where Shara Graustark (Jean Rogers) works. Blackstone gives the receipt to a henchman, Marker (Max Hoffman, Jr.), who hides it in the frame of a painting. X-9 captures Blackstone and sets out after Marker, who gets away in a speedboat. X-9 gives chase, and a fight breaks out. The boat goes out of control.

Chapter No. 2: "The Ray That Blinds" opens with a crash. The harbor police rescue both men. Meanwhile Baron Karsten visits Shara Graustark and then leaves for police headquarters, where Blackstone is released on a technicality. X-9 brings in his prisoner, Marker. Marker is killed in an escape attempt.

Pidge (David Oliver) and X-9 (Scott Kolk) capture villains (including Lon Chaney, Jr.) in this tense scene from *Secret Agent X-9.*

Blackstone and his gang head for the gallery. Shara Graustark is taken captive. X-9 arrives, unties Shara and pursues the villains. Using a ray-beam device, Blackstone blinds X-9 and another agent, Pidge (David Oliver), whose auto crashes.

Chapter No. 3: "The Man of Many Faces" finds X-9 and Pidge rescued by fellow agents. Another agent, Tommy Dawson (Henry Hunter) trails a shipment of paintings. Shara tosses a painting into the bushes along a roadside; Baron Karsten appears to seize it. X-9 and Pidge follow the Baron, who discards the painting. Pidge searches for the painting as X-9 and the Baron head toward the estate of the wealthy Raymond family. X-9 discovers that Mr. Raymond has been murdered. Pidge has found the painting. Karsten attempts to leave but is attacked en route by X-9. Karsten's auto smashes into a descending spiked gate, and X-9 is ejected.

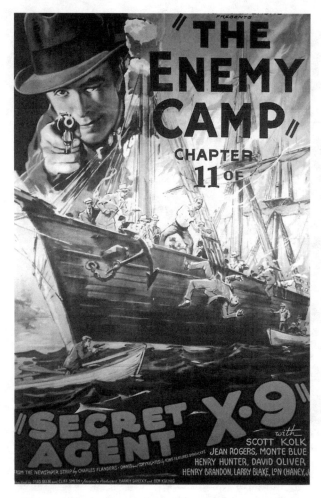

"The Listening Shadow" finds the gate machinery halted just inches away from impaling X-9. Pidge informs X-9 of the whereabouts of the painting. An agent of the thief known as Brenda overhears the conversation. A wild chase follows. X-9 and Tommy Dawson reach the hiding place of the painting which has been located, but Brenda's forces attack. Then a gasoline tank explodes.

Chapter No. 5: "False Fires" opens with an escape for X-9 and Dawson. They head for a meeting with Shara Graustark. X-9 finds that the canvas has been slashed and the bank receipt is missing. X-9 sends Shara to the Raymond estate and follows her. There, Karsten has found the bank receipt, which will lead him to the jewels.

Before X-9 can stop Baron Karsten, Blackstone takes aim on the agent. Blackstone and the Baron escape. Pidge breaks in, and he and X-9 subdue the gangsters. Pidge informs X-9 that the bank receipt is hidden in a bookcase. X-9 pulls out a book—which is rigged to trigger a revolver. The gun fires, and X-9 drops to the floor!

Chapter No. 6: "The Dragnet" reveals that Pidge has shoved X-9 out of the way just in time. Pidge is wounded. A double-crossing thug named Ransom (Leonard Lord) recovers from the fight, finds the bank receipt and rushes away—with X-9 in pursuit. Blackstone learns the vault's location from Karsten and hurries to recover the stolen goods.

But Blackstone finds only junk in the deposit box. He is interrupted by the G-Men, who chase Blackstone to an apartment building. A fight breaks out. The last thing we see is a body smashing through a window and plummeting earthward.

Chapter No. 7: "Sealed Lips" shows that one of Blackstone's men has fallen through the window. Blackstone and his gangsters flee. One of the crooks, captured by G-Men, agrees to tell where the elusive Brenda can be found. But before he can talk, he is murdered.

Brenda, in disguise as the Baron, walks coolly into the government offices to claim the jewels. Chief Agent Wheeler (Larry Blake) sends Tommy Dawson and the other federal men to accompany the supposed Baron to his embassy. Secret Agent X-9, Pidge and Shara follow. Spotting them, Brenda pushes Dawson out of the moving vehicle, into the path of the approaching car. Pidge swerves and hits a tree.

Chapter No. 8: "Exhibit A" begins with the collision, which proves nonfatal to all concerned. Dawson has managed to hold onto the jewels. Brenda, in a panic, has driven away. Visiting a suspicious-looking shop, X-9 is attacked but sends his assailant crashing backwards. The hoodlum falls into a loaded harpoon gun, and the missile seems to pin X-9 to the wall.

Chapter No. 9: "The Masquerader" shows that the harpoon has nailed only X-9's coat. Blackstone, hiding in a back room, rushes away with the captive Baron Karsten. Pidge frees X-9, who questions the shop owner. Pidge tracks down a tied-up Brenda, still in disguise as Baron Karsten. Pidge frees the crook and takes him into custody.

X-9 boards an old-fashioned pirate ship, which is now used as a public attraction. The ship doubles as a mob hideout. X-9 is overcome and beaten. The thugs have captured the real Baron Karsten; they take off in a speedboat. Tommy Dawson and X-9 use a speedboat to follow the crooks. Dawson has to maneuver the boat between a pier and a freighter, and it doesn't look as though he'll make it through.

Chapter No. 10: "The Forced Lie" proves Dawson to be a very good speedboat pilot. He and X-9 continue after the gangsters and the kidnapped Baron Karsten. The thugs make it to shore ahead of X-9 and Dawson and head out toward the Raymond estate. X-9 and Dawson take a shortcut. There is another fight against the jewel thieves. X-9 helps to

GANGLAND KILLERS
BEWARE!

THIS MAN NEVER MISSES!

Secret Agent X-9 the heroic G-Man who thrilled millions in the famous newspaper cartoon strip now battles his way through 12 nerve-tingling chapters on the screen!

Secret Agent X-9

with SCOTT KOLK
JEAN ROGERS
MONTE BLUE
HENRY HUNTER
DAVID OLIVER
HENRY BRANDON

From the newspaper strip by Charles Flanders owned and copyrighted by King Features Syndicate

A NEW, UNIVERSAL CHAPTER PLAY.

free the real Baron Karsten but finds that the disguised Brenda has probably already reached the embassy.

Brenda moves to claim the jewels. However, Shara Graustark has seen through the disguise and gets the drop on the master thief. Brenda shoots Shara's revolver out of her hand and escapes. Shara and Pidge follow. Pidge shoots out a tire on Brenda's car. Shara's car plunges over a cliff.

Chapter No. 11: "The Enemy Camp" finds the rear tires of Shara's car still safely on the roadway. Back at the Raymond estate, Brenda is again surrounded by government agents but kills Tom Dawson and escapes. X-9 and Pidge head toward the pirate ship. The crooks are prepared for them. X-9 falls into the water.

Chapter No. 12: "Crime Does Not Pay" opens with Pidge rescuing X-9. Agents swarm over the ship, and the surviving crooks surrender. Brenda, still disguised as Baron Karsten, escapes. At another hideout, Blackstone finds the jewel box empty. There follows a confrontation with a crooked go-between named Delaney (Robert Kortman). Finally, X-9 breaks in and declares: "That's all we need, Blackstone—the admission that you are Brenda!" The jewels are returned, and the serial ends as Shara smiles lovingly at Secret Agent X-9.

Chief villain Henry Brandon gave film scholar Gregory Mank a rather rancorous view of Lon Chaney, Jr.:

I knew Chaney when he was a bit player. We had an expression, the second man through the door, which meant the villain's henchman, the guy who does the physical job—when the villain snaps his fingers, the second man through the door jumps and throttles somebody. That was Chaney at this time.

Chaney was very bitter, and rather mean. Once, on *Secret Agent X-9*, he said to me, "You know, the rest of us are getting pretty fed up with you... You blow your lines in the long shots so you can get close-ups!" That had never occurred to me. I said, "I blew the lines because we haven't had enough rehearsal, but by the time we get to the close-ups, I know the lines." I found him rather disagreeable, but it was fun to debate with him.

Photographs from the production show Chaney looking antagonistic, usually in the company of Brandon and other villainous players.

When at last Chaney got the stage role part of a childlike brute in *Of Mice and Men*, he wisely connected with Wallace Ford, who had appeared opposite Broderick Crawford in the East Coast production of the play. Ford generously helped Junior learn the role. Meanwhile, Henry Brandon gradually found himself on friendlier terms with Chaney. Brandon told Greg Mank:

Chaney and I had always had an ongoing argument: He felt an actor didn't need stage experience. I had mostly stage experience, and we had this constant debate going on between us... Well, about the second week of [the West Coast] *Of Mice and Men*, I went to see it. Chaney had gotten very good reviews, and after the performance I went backstage and knocked on his dressing room door, ready to remind him of our old debate... [H]e yelled, "Don't say, I told you so!"...

Actor Russell Wade told me that Chaney was more impressive in the stage version than in the film. "He was excellent in it!" Wade said. "He was excellent on the stage!" The conventional wisdom still holds that Junior was an actor of only limited range, and that much of his success stemmed from his being the son of an acknowledged great actor. Wade said, in rebuttal, that this is only a natural—however unfair—conclusion. Wade remarked:

> He hadn't proved himself and he hadn't done anything for people to think differently. He doesn't talk a hell of a lot [in *Of Mice and Men*]. He was a good man, and he set everybody on their ear when he did that show in Hollywood, because they really came up and noticed him. It got good reviews.

After half a decade of scrambling, Lon Chaney, Jr. was finally on his way. People—and not just *people*, but the *right people*—were beginning to take notice.

CREDITS: Directors: Ford Beebe and Cliff Smith; Story and Screenplay by Wyndham Gittens, Norman S. Hall, Ray Trampe and Leslie Swabacher; from the King Features Comic Strip; a Serial in 12 Chapters; Released: February 11, 1937

CAST: Scott Kolk (Secret Agent X-9); Jean Rogers (Shara Groustark); Monte Blue (Baron Karsten); David Oliver (Pidge); Larry Blake (Wheeler); Henry Brandon (Blackstone); Lon Chaney, Jr. (Maroni); Henry Hunter (Tommy Dawson); Bentley Hewlett (Scarlett); George Shelley (Packard); Robert Dalton (Thurston); Leonard Lord (Ransom); Robert Kortman (Delaney); Edward Piel, Sr. (Fence); Lynn Gilbert (Rose); William Royle (Dunn); Eddy C. Walker (Attorney); Douglas Edwards (Henchman); Max Hoffman, Jr. (Marker); Ed Parker and Tom Steele (Stunt Doubles)

CHAPTER TITLES: 1) "Modern Pirates"; 2) "The Ray That Blinds"; 3) "The Man of Many Faces"; 4) "The Listening Shadow"; 5) "False Fires"; 6) "The Dragnet"; 7) "Sealed Lips"; 8) "Exhibit A"; 9) "The Masquerader"; 10) "The Forced Lie"; 11) "The Enemy Camp"; 12) "Crime Does Not Pay"

RIDERS OF DEATH VALLEY
(Universal Pictures Corp.; 1941)

Universal's publicity department hyped *Riders of Death Valley* as a breakthrough million-dollar serial. This was quite so, in a sense, but the big-ticket sum referred more to the extravagant salaries of the star-player cast than to any remarkable production values. Given the assembled talents, *Riders* looks like nothing quite so much as a missed opportunity.

The prominent heroes of *Riders of Death Valley*: Tombstone (Buck Jones), Jim Benton (Dick Foran), Pancho (Leo Carillo), Smokey (Noah Beery, Jr.) and Borax Bill (Guinn "Big Boy" Williams).

Lon Chaney, Jr. and Charles Bickford put the bad in bad men in *Riders of Death Valley*.

Co-director Ford Beebe, Sr. would have relished the opportunity to fashion a better story in keeping with the wealth of star-caliber names: "Had we known the kind of players we would have, we could have written a serial that would have been worthy of their individual talents," he told *Screen Facts* magazine.

Ford Beebe, Jr. has told me that Universal was more keenly interested in quantity than in quality.

> I'm not so sure that the people who worked on [the serials] weren't trying to turn out a decent product, but the front office was strictly financially geared... [T]he front

A behind-the-scenes publicity shot of Jeanne Kelly strumming a guitar as Monte Blue and Lon Chaney, Jr. listen during *Riders of Death Valley*.

office never thought they needed [a good story]. [Serials] were a series of episodes where people get into trouble, and so why do you need a story? My Dad was always soap-boxing the point that he had trouble developing anything if he didn't have a structure to it. That was a beef with him, always.

It was not entirely the explosions and crashes and cliffhanger chapter endings that brought the kids into the theaters, week after week. In a *Flash Gordon* serial, kids cared about what would happen to the characters. The outer-space plot is outlandish, but the characters lend it an identifiably human dimension. The story and characterizations on which *Riders of Death Valley* hangs are, on the other hand, fundamentally hollow.

That the serial has proved itself memorable owes more to its pageant of once-famous cowboy heroes than to any compelling drama or sharply defined fictional characters.

To compensate for the shortcomings of the script, directors Beebe and Taylor seem to have encouraged the cast to ad-lib whenever necessary. This was done to give some dimension to their characters, adding to the overall enjoyment of this serial.

Riders of Death Valley hinges on the adventures of Jim Benton (Dick Foran) and a group of fun-loving cowboys—among them, Tombstone (Buck Jones), Borax Bill (Guinn "Big Boy" Williams), Pancho (Leo Carillo), Smokey (Noah Beery, Jr.)—who fight the villains who would take over the peaceful town of Panamint. The chief bad guys are Joseph Kirby (James Blaine) and Rance Davis (Monte Blue), who pose as respected citizens. Kirby and Davis prefer to do their dirty work under cover. They maintain an uneasy alliance with Wolf Reade (Charles Bickford) and his henchmen Butch (Lon Chaney, Jr.), Pete (Richard Alexander) and Rusty (Ethan Laidlaw), among other thugs. The villains resent Jim Benton, for a miner named Chuckawalla Charlie Morgan (Frank Austin) has found new deposits in a supposedly played-out mine and has named Jim as a partner.

Chuckawalla has willed his share to his niece, Mary Morgan (Jeanne Kelly, later known as Jean Brooks). The crooks at one point try to present a fake Mary Morgan when the time comes for the niece to assert her claim.

Mary is en route on a stagecoach that Morgan and Davis have set up for a Reade gang holdup. When the stagecoach veers out of control, Jim tries to rescue Mary. However, the truer hero turns out to be Buck Jones' Tombstone, a wisecracking, hard-charging *hombre* whose fascinating presence owes more to Jones' own personality than to any savvy writing of the role. Through the many adventures—explosions, dust storms, shoot-outs—Jim Benton and company always come through, and in the end they rout any number of villains, save the mine and rescue the town.

The story—such as it is—is not bad for run-of-the-mill horse-opera fare. The exceptional cast, however, deserved better, and the same goes for their fans. On the plus side, the very players seem to have improvised a great deal of their banter and tough talk on the spot.

Riders had been scheduled for production before Universal developed the bright idea to make it an all-star serial. In the haste of retooling

Butch (Lon Chaney, Jr.) appears ready to sneak up on one of the good guys in *Riders of Death Valley*.

the project, the studio neglected to consider the need for a massive re-write, to re-tailor the generic material to the caliber of players involved.

Nevertheless, the actors made the best of it. Even in a small scene, Lon Chaney, Jr. can be seen to throw in that little something extra. Junior works extremely well with chief villain Charles Bickford. In one scene, Chaney decides he must prove his worth to the boss: Chaney and fellow

A scene from a lobby card where main heroes and villains (including Charles Bickford and Lon Chaney, Jr.) are all together and smiling in *Riders of Death Valley*.

henchman Dick Alexander have cornered heroic Dick Foran on a mountain crag. Alexander warns Chaney that their master wants the captive alive. "This is one time I'm forgettin' orders!" insists Chaney. "...That *hombre*'s given us too much trouble already! We'll call this an *accident*!"

In his 1933 interview with *Movie Classic* magazine, Chaney told Nancy Pryor:

> I don't exactly know my true screen place yet... I sometimes think I would like to do Westerns. Maybe that is because I'm not quite sure of myself as an actor ... and not an awful lot of acting ability is required for Westerns.

Chalk that remark up to youthful naiveté: By the time of *Riders of Death Valley*, Chaney had learned that all acting requires hard work and immersion in character, with or without the advantage of carefully developed scriptwriting. Even in this lesser role, Chaney shows not only an emerging intensity of screen presence but also a willingness to bring to the role more than has been written for him to enact. Coupled with Junior's soulfully intense stare and a brusquely enthusiastic manner of speech,

Lon Chaney, Jr. shows Jeanne Kelly (left) and another actress how to roll a cigarette on the set of *Riders of Death Valley*. (Photofest)

even the conventional bad-guy dialogue comes across with an intimidating ferocity.

The casting is uniformly spectacular: Singer-actor Dick Foran had been popular at Warner Bros. in the mid-1930s; he fared well, too, at Universal, where he registered strongly in *The Mummy's Hand* and the serial *Winners of the West* (both 1940). Buck Jones is as good naturedly self-assured, even to the point of benevolent arrogance, as he had been in his heyday of a decade and more past. Though he required extensive stunt-doubling at age 53, Jones remained a commanding presence. Jones died in a nightclub fire in 1942 while touring on behalf of U.S. Defense Bonds.

Leo Carillo's character prefigures the *Cisco Kid* movies. Even the smaller parts are played impressively by the likes of Glenn Strange, Roy

Barcroft and Edmund Cobb. The fights and chases are well done, whether staged from scratch or edited in from stock footage.

The musical score is top-notch, and many fans still remember the haunting classical strains of Mendelssohn's *Fingals' Cave Overture*, along with bits of Frank Skinner's score from *Destry Rides Again* (1939) and fragments from Universal's stock library.

The crowning touch may well be the rich show of villainy, particularly from Charles Bickford and Lon Chaney, Jr. who had of course worked together shortly beforehand in *Of Mice and Men*. Never mind that this serial comes nowhere near that level: It's often the singer, and not the song itself, that really counts.

The *Motion Picture Herald* weighed in on a favorable note in its April 12, 1941, issue: "Production values abound in this serial... There is ample evidence to support Universal's claim that it is 'a million-dollar super serial.' While the story is somewhat familiar, the first three chapters, at least, move along at a fast pace and are likely to please the serial addict. Direction, acting and production mounting are in keeping with the star-studded cast. This serial offers immense possibilities for selling and should be a drawing card for the weekend juvenile trade; also for the many adults who get a kick out of action films."

CREDITS: Associate Producer: Henry MacRae; Directors: Ford Beebe and Ray Taylor; Screenplay: Sherman Lowe, George Plympton, Basil Dickey and Jack Connell; Story: Oliver Drake; Photography: Jerome Ash and William Sickner; Music: Excerpts of Felix Mendelssohn's *Fingals' Cave Overture* and Cues from Frank Skinner's *Destry Rides Again* Score; a Serial in 15 Chapters; Released: March 6, 1941

CAST: Dick Foran (Jim Benton), Leo Carillo (Pancho), Buck Jones (Tombstone), Charles Bickford (Wolf Reade), Lon Chaney, Jr. (Butch), Noah Beery, Jr. (Smokey), Guinn "Big Boy" Williams (Borax Bill), Jeanne Kelly [aka Jean Brooks] (Mary Morgan), James Blaine (Joseph Kirby), Monte Blue (Rance Davis), Glenn Strange (Tex), Roy Barcroft (Dick), Ethan Laidlaw (Rusty), Dick Alexander (Pete), Jack Rockwell (Trigger), Frank Austin (Chuckawalla), Charles Thomas (Rimrock), William Hall (Gordon), James Guilfoyle (Judge Knox), Ernie Adams (Cactus), Edmund Cobb (Salty), William Pagan (Marshal), Jack Clifford (Lafe Hogan), Richard Travis (Joe Miller), Jack Perrin (Guard), Ivar

McFadden (Bragg), Jerome Harte (Richards), Ruth Rickaby (Kate), Don Rowan (Blake), Bud Osborne (Stage Driver), Slim Whitaker (Ira Jackson), Frank Brownlee (Slim), Art Miles (Evergreene), Ed Payson (Buck Hansen), James Farley (Graham), Alonzo Price (Wilson), Ted Adams (Hank), Dick Rush (Bartender), Kim Nolan and Jay Michaels (Cashiers), Gil Perkins (Fighter), Duke York (Stunt Double), James Lucas (Bartender) and Silver (Buck Jones' horse, doubled by horses Sandy and Eagle)

CHAPTER TITLES: 1) "Death Marks the Trail!"; 2) "The Menacing Herd!"; 3) "The Plunge of Peril!"; 4) "Flaming Fury!"; 5) "The Avalanche of Doom!"; 6) "Blood and Gold!"; 7) "Death Rides the Storm!"; 8) "Descending Doom!"; 9) "Death Holds the Reins!"; 10) "Devouring Flames!"; 11) "The Fatal Blast!"; 12) "Thundering Doom!"; 13) "The Bridge of Disaster!"; 14) "A Fight to the Death!"; 15) "The Harvest of Hate!"

OVERLAND MAIL
(Universal Pictures Corp.; 1942)

After a terrific shoot-out, outlaw Sam Gregg (Harry Cording) is taken to the town doctor. The doctor tells good guys Jim Lane (Lon Chaney, Jr.), Buckskin Bill (Don Terry) and Sierra (Noah Beery, Jr.) that Gregg is probably not going to pull through. Gregg opens his eyes and calls to Jim Lane. "Take it easy, Gregg!," says Lane. "The doc says you gotta rest!"

Gregg protests: "I heard what the doc said. I'm cashin' in my chips!... you want me to tell you who I've been workin' for, don't you?"

"That sure would help a lot!" replies Lane.

Gregg pauses significantly, then: "Well, I ain't gonna tell you nothin'!"

Gregg dies. The look of anger and disgust that crosses Lane's face shows the controlled subtlety and strength that had become part and parcel of a Chaney, Jr. performance.

In 1942, shortly after *Overland Mail* was completed, Ford Beebe the younger visited his dad on the set of *Son of Dracula*. Ford I. Beebe, Jr. met Chaney on a few occasions, and he shared with me his memories of the encounters:

A sneering Jim Lane (Lon Chaney, Jr.) from *Overland Mail*.

Well, he was a little self-contained. I don't
mean at all egotistical. But certainly not a

An interesting shot of heroes and villains together: Barbara Gilbert (Helen Parrish), Jim Lane, Tom Gilbert (Tom Chatterton), Sheriff Tyler (Jack Clifford), Frank Chadwick (Noah Beery, Sr.), Sierra Pete (Noah Beery, Jr.), Buckskin Bill (Don Terry), and unknown actor, from *Overland Mail*.

back-slapper, but he was very nice—very friendly guy. I never socialized with him after work, or anything. In fact, I guess I talked with him only three or four times. Just to say, hello, going by...

Truthfully, he—off the screen...—was a lot like he was on camera. I mean, he was not too expressive unless... well, in a picture, he would usually have... some psychological part. He never was a leading

Iron Eyes Cody teaches Helen Parrish and Lon Chaney, Jr. how to properly shoot a bow and arrow in this publicity from *Overland Mail*.

man or anything like that—I mean in the sense of a romantic lead. His facial features and everything tended to be sort of

Jim Lane and Sierra are captured by Indians in *Overland Mail*.

unexpressive, you know? And he was very much like that to look at off the screen. But if you talked to him, he'd brighten up—if it called for it—and, as I say, he was quite friendly. I think he probably could have appreciated a couple more friends himself. He struck you as a kind of person who didn't know how to go about being appreciated.

With *Son of Dracula*, Junior now had to prove himself worthy of inheriting a role that Bela Lugosi had defined beyond challenge. The aloof stoicism of the role may have colored the off-screen presence that Beebe, Jr. encountered. We keep running across the notion of an

Barbara Gilbert listens as Jim Lane has a frank discussion with Tom Gilbert (Tom Chatterton) about the problems he's been having in *Overland Mail*.

unexpressive face in accounts of Chaney's life and work. Probably, the most unexpressive image of Chaney is his performance as the Monster in *The Ghost of Frankenstein* (1942)—whose very screenplay reveals that Chaney was instructed to play the Monster precisely so. Of course, Chaney's face is highly expressive as the villainous Butch in *Riders of Death Valley* and likewise as the tough but warm-hearted Jim Lane in *Overland Mail*. George E. Turner appraised the popular perception of Chaney in these words: "Those who say Junior's face was unexpressive were nuts. His pantomime and facial expressions were always good. His voice sometimes wasn't appropriate."

Overland Mail hangs on the device of a million-dollar mail contract offered by the U.S. government. Tom Gilbert's Overland Mail Co. is

Another great publicity shot of Don Terry, Helen Parrish, Lon Chaney, Jr. and Noah Beery, Jr. in *Overland Mail.*

assured of the contract. But Gilbert (Tom Chatterton) has failed to reckon with the greed of a friendly rival, Frank Chadwick (a gentlemanly Noah Beery, Sr.). Chadwick conspires to land the contract by treacherous means.

Chadwick hires a bunch of hooligans, including Charles Darson (Robert Barron), Sam Gregg (Harry Cording) and a half-breed Indian called the Puma (Charles Stevens). Frank Chadwick keeps up a front of friendly innocence. Special Agent Jim Lane smells a rat and responds accordingly. Lane is attracted to Barbara Gilbert (Helen Parrish), the boss' daughter.

The source-author, Johnston McCulley, is better known as the creator of Zorro, the populist hero who originated in *All Story Weekly* magazine in 1919. Douglas Fairbanks, captivated by the character, undertook

Everyone is impressed by Frank Chadwick's (Noah Beery, Sr.) suggestions except Jim Lane (Lon Chaney, Jr.) in *Overland Mail.*

to produce, co-write and enact the title role in 1920's *The Mark of Zorro*, which features Noah Beery, Sr., as a comical villain.

The most impressive quality about *Overland Mail* is its conversational dialogue, which invites a natural sincerity from Chaney and his supporting players. Helen Parrish makes an ideal romantic interest for Junior—a beauty, with intelligence and resilience. It is a rarity that a leading man in a serial seems so evenly matched with a leading lady.

No one, for that matter, seems to give a half-hearted performance. Noah Beery, Sr. makes an unusually dignified villain. His son, Noah, Jr. is right in his element as the hero's best friend. Radio actor Jackson Beck told me:

Lon Chaney, Jr. and Helen Parrish display terrific on-screen chemistry in *Overland Mail*. **(Photofest)**

> Man, I gotta tell you that Noah Beery, Jr.
> was exactly like his father, Noah Beery,
> Sr. They were as alike as two peas in a
> pod... exactly alike, delivery, everything!
> [Beery] Junior did heavies too, for awhile,
> until they found out he was a great second
> banana.

Ford Beebe and John Rawlins directed *Overland Mail*. According to Ford Beebe, Jr., his dad and Rawlins didn't always agree as to the proper approach, but their collaboration here possesses a fine consistency of

Ten years after *The Last Frontier*, Lon Chaney, Jr. again played a hero this time in *Overland Mail*.

style. Rawlins had entered the movies as a stuntman and actor, primarily in action-adventure films and serials. In the 1930s, he wrote gags for comedy shorts and served Columbia Pictures as a film editor. By 1938 he had become a director, a field in which he would remain active for the next 20 years. Among his films are *Sherlock Holmes and the Voice of Terror* and *Arabian Nights* (both 1942) and *Dick Tracy Meets Gruesome* (1947), with Ralph Byrd and Boris Karloff.

While Boris had his heroic role in *The Hope Diamond Mystery* and Bela had *The Return of Chandu*, Chaney, Jr. had *Overland Mail*. His relaxed performance is light years away from his similar part in *The Last Frontier*. Jim Lane is undoubtedly one of Chaney, Jr.'s most enjoyable performances.

Too bad that *Overland Mail* marked Chaney's last real crack at playing a rugged, heroic leading man. Fans can scarcely do better than to catch his act as a brutal henchman in *Riders of Death Valley* and at his heroic best in *Overland Mail*. These two, coupled with his better-known feature-film leads, establish beyond question that Lon Chaney, Jr. was a great deal more than just the son of the Man of a Thousand Faces.

CREDITS: Associate Producer: Henry MacRae; Directors: Ford Beebe and John Rawlins; Screenplay: Paul Huston; Story: Johnston McCulley; Photographed by: William Sickner and George Robinson; Art Director: Harold H. MacArthur; Dialogue Director: Jacques Jaccard; Edited by: Alvin Todd, Louis Sackin, Joseph H. Glick and Patrick Kelley; Supervising Editor: Saul A. Goodkind; Western Electric Sound; Music: Excerpts from Frank Skinner's *Destry Rides Again* score, among others; a Serial in 15 Chapters; Released: June 12, 1942

CAST: Lon Chaney, Jr. (Jim Lane); Helen Parrish (Barbara Gilbert); Noah Beery, Jr. (Sierra Pete); Don Terry ("Buckskin" Bill Burke); Bob Baker (Young Bill Cody); Noah Beery, Sr. (Frank Chadwick); Tom Chatterton (Tom Gilbert); Charles Stevens (Puma); Robert Barron (Charles Darson); Harry Cording (Sam Gregg); Marguerite De La Motte [given elsewhere as De La Motta] (Rose); Ben Taggart (Lamont); Jack Rockwell (Slade); Roy Harris [aka Riley Hill] (Lem); Carleton Young (Jake); Jack Clifford (Sheriff Tyler); Chief Many Treaties (Black Cloud); Chief Thundercloud (Chief Many Moons); Tom Steele (Express Rider); William Gould (Colonel Malford); Frank Pershing (Captain Hinton); Forrest Taylor (Taylor); Bill Moss (Briston); Ruth Rickaby (Minnie); Charles Phipps (Dr. Burnside); Eddie Polo (Pioneer); Frosty Royce (Landue); George Sherwood (Lieutenant Turner); Dave O' Donnell (Orderly); Jack Shannon (Man); Henry Wills (Indian, Townsman and Wagon Driver); Henry Hall (Crabtree Wagon Leader); Charles Murphy (Wrangler and Townsman); Al Taylor and Curley Dresden (Café Patrons); Blackie Whiteford (Bartender); Ray Teal (Dying Indian); William Desmond (Williams, a Banker, and Man at Barricade); Artie Ortego (Indian); Blackjack Ward (Man Holding Reins); Iron Eyes Cody (Indian); and Art Dillard and Tex Palmer (Townsmen)

CHAPTER TITLES: 1) "A Race With Disaster!"; 2) "Flaming Havoc!"; 3) "The Menacing Herd!"; 4) "The Bridge of Disaster!"; 5) "Hurled to the Depths!"; 6) "Death at the Stake!"; 7) "The Path of Peril!"; 8) "Imprisoned in Flames!"; 9) "Hidden Danger!"; 10) "Blazing Wagons!"; 11) "The Trail of Terror!"; 12) "In the Claws of the Cougar!"; 13) "The Frenzied Mob!"; 14) "The Toll of Treachery!"; 15) "The Mail Goes Through!"

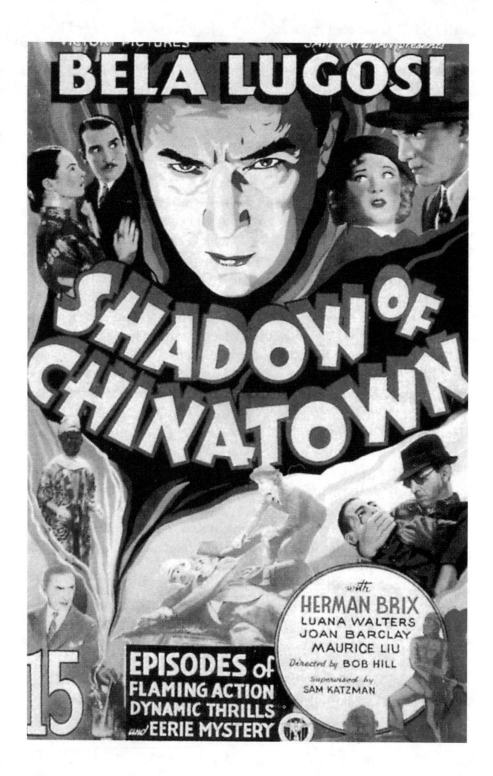

BELA LUGOSI

VICTORY PICTURES

SAM KATZMAN presents

SHADOW OF CHINATOWN

15

EPISODES of
FLAMING ACTION
DYNAMIC THRILLS
and EERIE MYSTERY

with
HERMAN BRIX
LUANA WALTERS
JOAN BARCLAY
MAURICE LIU
Directed by **BOB HILL**
Supervised by
SAM KATZMAN

CHAPTER SIX
Boris, Bela & Lon, Jr.
The Final Chapter

Boris Karloff may have looked at his serials with a certain amount of nostalgia, but as he told interviewers George E. Turner and Michael H. Price in 1968, he was grateful that those days were long since past. Bela Lugosi likely regarded his serials as makeshift passages through hard times. For Lon Chaney, Jr. the serials reveal the truest portrait of his career between 1932 to 1942, going from an awkward and insecure but hard-working actor to a true professional.

Chaney's last serial even allowed him the role of a romantic leading man, almost of the sort he had only *hoped* to play in his slightly later *Inner Sanctum* series. That string of half-a-dozen offbeat mysteries was given the lowest of budgets, and Universal cast Chaney more for peculiarity's sake than for his natural appeal. Lon often admitted his frustration with a studio that—except for his tailor-made role as the Wolf Man—didn't prepare interesting characters for him, or even cast him in films that would have challenged his skills.

Boris Karloff certainly made his share of inferior movies over the long stretch, but he could look with pride at his body of work. Actor Russell Wade remembers watching Karloff and Lugosi at work together when he was starting out in the business—possibly on the set of *The Invisible Ray* (1936)—and later, of course, in *The Body Snatcher* (1945): "They didn't get along too well. But it didn't show. They both did their jobs! They were very nice. That's all I can say! Karloff was a great actor, in spite of all those horror pictures that he made. I don't know about Lugosi. They both were very professional. They knew their lines… [The studios] were smart in putting them together, because they played well [together]…"

Kate Phillips knew Boris fairly well in the Hollywood of the late 1930s and early 1940s. Mrs. Phillips was then known as actress Kay Linaker. She tells this story:

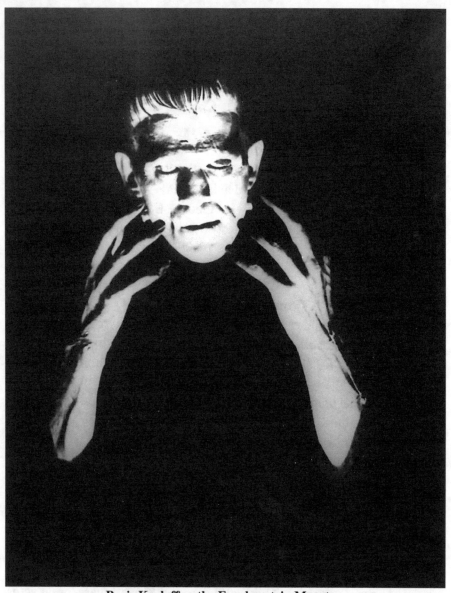

Boris Karloff as the Frankenstein Monster.

I knew Boris when he was living in Brentwood, and I think his daughter [Sara] was maybe 4 at the time this happened. One day, he took the dogs—he had those Bedlingtons [Bedlington terriers]—and he took them for a little walk, down the back of the property and down to the next street. And when he did, a man was ambling down the street, and the dogs ran toward him, and they barked. And Boris called them back, and the man came up to him, and he said, "Do me a favor!" He was very drunk! He said, "Can you take me, please, to the Cedars of Lebanon hospital, right now? Because I realize that I need help! I'm in a bad way!"

Boris asked him, "What makes you think you need help?" [The man said:] "I just saw three sheep bark!" "So," Boris said, as he was telling the story, "I tried very hard to explain that to him that they were not black sheep, they were dogs," and the man took it that he was rejecting him and not taking care of his really serious situation. I said, "What did you do?" He said, "What could I do? I took him to the hospital!" He [Boris] was a dear!

Had Lugosi regained his health and lived only a few years longer, his unexpected movies-on-television fame might have helped him come to terms with Karloff. The revival of the Depression-into-wartime Universal films certainly invigorated the careers of Karloff and Chaney.

Bela Lugosi, Jr. reveals some favorite memories of his father:

> ...I remember his being very conscientious with his work. Very demanding of himself, as an artist. Taking pride in his work. Being impatient with those who flubbed scenes, and who would not bring themselves up to the quality of acting that he thought ought to be given by a performer.
>
> My Dad never did compromise his— his quality. He was a great artist and a great actor, in my estimation. I think he realized

Bela Lugosi in the stage production of *Dracula*.

his powers over people, his magnetism. I just remember observing him. I was just fascinated with the reaction of others to my father. Everybody remembered him! They *had* to! I could just see his influence over people. Although I wasn't too aware of what was happening at the time, I think

> now that he had probably a tremendous
> appeal to women. He had a powerful voice,
> a style about him, which I wish I had.

There were times that Karloff and Lugosi were friendly, especially during the festive occasion that was the making of *Son of Frankenstein* in 1938-39. On the other hand, the politics of casting on *Black Friday* (1940) and *The Invisible Ray* (1936) scarcely can have endeared Karloff to Lugosi.

One of the great mysteries surrounding the Karloff-plus-Lugosi mystique has been the question of what really happened to cause crucial last-minute changes in *Black Friday*. Karloff had balked at the Jekyll-and-Hyde character that ended up being played by Stanley Ridges. Karloff, instead, wanted to play the renegade-surgeon role, which clearly had been for Bela Lugosi. As things turned out, Lugosi landed a small role as a gangster—who never meets Karloff's character on-screen. Karloff's daughter, Sara Jane, has candidly noted that Lugosi must have been furious about the strange change in casting.

> Personal life had nothing to do with it. It
> would be very understandable if Bela were
> jealous of my father's professional life.

Lon Chaney, Jr. remains the most complex and problematical personality of the three leading horror-movie stars. By the early 1940s, Chaney's character from *Of Mice and Men* had already been caricatured in animated cartoons along with Karloff's Monster and Lugosi's Dracula. It wasn't until the 1970s that the Wolf Man would be animated on TV cartoons such as *The Groovy Ghoulies*.

Director Reginald LeBorg, who often worked with Chaney, Jr., once posed this question, "If Lon Chaney, Jr. had not had so famous a father, could he have achieved stardom?" This is indeed an arbitrary thought because stardom depends not only upon talent but also on opportunity. Junior was never given the opportunity on his own; it all had to do with whether the industry recognized him as the son of Lon Chaney.

There are too many conflicting stories as to how the three men got along with each other. Director Reginald LeBorg has said that Lugosi and Chaney didn't get along during the making of *The Black Sleep* (1956).

Claude Rains and Lon Chaney, Jr. in *The Wolf Man.*

However, Hope L. Lugosi, Bela's last wife, said that Lon, Jr. was the one actor Bela respected and admired out of the entire cast, which also included John Carradine, Basil Rathbone, Tor Johnson and Akim Tamiroff.

How did Karloff and Chaney, Jr. get along? Instead of conflicting stories, we have very little at all to go on. Certainly, in many interviews, Karloff made a point of praising Junior's father, and on a record album called *An Evening with Boris Karloff and His Friends* (1966), he said that Junior's work in *The Wolf Man* would have "done credit to his dad."

Although Susanna Foster found Boris Karloff cold during the making of *The Climax* (1944), she thought Chaney was a wonderful man. Perhaps Karloff was unhappy with his one-dimensional character and a patch of domestic strife, and couldn't hide his disappointment from his fellow actors. David Manners spoke of Lugosi as an annoyance, but many others have characterized Lugosi as a terrific person and a dedicated actor. The point of all this is that these actors were human beings, and they had their good days and bad days.

The horror movies—or to use Karloff's more genteel term, thrillers—of Boris Karloff, Bela Lugosi and Lon Chaney, Jr. are crucial to the cultural heritage. Their most famous characters are now part of American mythology. While the films' power to frighten have diminished with age, the respect for the actors and technicians can only gather in momentum.

The serials that Boris, Bela and Junior made are also crucial to this legacy. They are best viewed in context with the stars' better-known work.

For the Karloff fans, a chapter or two of *King of the Wild* will go well as a prelude to *Frankenstein* or *The Mummy*. Followers of Lugosi's work could do worse than to run an episode or two of *The Return of Chandu* with *The Black Cat* or the very serial-like *The Raven*. Chaney's will enjoy a chapter or two of *Undersea Kingdom* with *Of Mice and Men* or *The Wolf Man* or—just to stray from the overfamiliar—*The Alligator People*. You might enjoy the crueler side of Chaney in *Riders of Death Valley* or the more heroic side of him in *Overland Mail*—just a chapter or two, for an appetizer—with *Son of Dracula* or *Strange Confession*.

Those who are just now discovering the serials will do well to remember that they hardly bear viewing in a single sitting. What they do bear is a willingness to rediscover a form of entertainment that kept generations enthralled from the dawning of World War II to the early stages of the Cold War. If the viewer's fondness for Karloff, Lugosi or Chaney leads to a greater appreciation of a cinematic idiom that often goes unacknowledged, then our popular culture will be all the richer for it.

BIBLIOGRAPHY

Barbour, Alan G., *Cliffhanger: A Pictorial History of the Motion Picture Serial*. Secaucus, NJ, Citadel Press, 1977

Barbour, Alan G., *Saturday Afternoon at the Movies: 3 Volumes in One*, New York, Bonanza Books, 1986

Beck, Calvin Thomas, *Heroes of the Horrors*, New York and London, Collier Books/Collier MacMillian, Publishers, Ltd., 1975

Bojarski, Richard, *The Films of Bela Lugosi*, Secaucus, NJ, Citadel Press, 1980

Bojarski, Richard and Kenneth Beale, *The Films of Boris Karloff*, Secaucus, NJ, Citadel Press, 1976

Brunas, Michael & John, and Tom Weaver, *Universal Horrors: The Studio's Classic Films, 1931-1946*, Jefferson, NC, and London, McFarland & Co., Inc., 1990

Coghlan, Frank "Junior," *They Still Call Me Junior: Autobiography of a Child Star*, Jefferson, NC, and London, McFarland & Co. Inc., 1993

Clarens, Carlos, *An Illustrated History of the Horror Film*, New York, Capricorn Books, 1967

Cline, William C., *In the Nick of Time: Motion Picture Sound Serials*. Jefferson, NC, and London, McFarland & Co., Inc., 1990

Cremer, Robert, *Lugosi: The Man Behind the Cape*, Chicago, Henry Regnery Co., 1978

Edwards, Colin, *Between the Bolts*, audiotape of radio interview with Boris Karloff, Karloff Enterprises, 1997

Everson, William K., *More Classics of the Horror Film: Fifty Years of Great Chillers*, Secaucus, NJ, Citadel Press, 1986

Fairbanks, Douglas, Jr., *Salad Days*, New York, Doubleday, 1988

Foy, Fred, Liner Notes for *The Smithsonian Collection: Old Time Radio Westerns: A Rare In-Depth Look at the History of Old Time Radio and the Western Story*, Washington, DC, Radio Spirits & Smithsonian Institution Press, 1996

Gifford, Denis, *Karloff: The Man, the Monster, the Movies*, New York, Curtis Books, 1973

Grey, Rudolph, *Nightmare of Ecstasy: The Life and Art of Edward D. Wood, Jr.*, Portland, OR, Feral House, 1992/94

Harmon, Jim and Donald F. Glut, *The Great Movie Serials: Their Sound and Fury*, New York, Doubleday & Co., Inc., 1972

Jensen, Paul M., *Boris Karloff and His Films*, Cranbury, NJ, A.S. Barnes & Co., Inc., 1974

Kinnard, Roy, *Fifty Years of Serial Thrills*, Metuchen, NJ and London, Scarecrow Press, 1983

Lahue, Kalton C., *Bound and Gagged: The Story of the Silent Serials*, Cranbury, N.J., A.S. Barnes & Co., 1968

Lahue, Kalton C., *Continued Next Week: A History of the Motion Picture Serial*, Norman, OK, University of Oklahoma Press, 1964

Lennig, Arthur, *The Count: The Life and Times of Bela "Dracula" Lugosi*, New York, G.P. Putnam's Sons, 1974

Mathis, Jack, *Valley of the Cliffhangers*, Barrington, IL, Jack Mathis Advertising, 1975

Mathis, Jack, *Valley of the Cliffhangers Supplement*, Barrington, IL, Jack Mathis Advertising, 1995

McCarthy, Kevin and Ed Gorman, eds. *"They're Here...", Invasion of the Body Snatchers: A Tribute*, New York, Berkley Boulevard Books, 1999

Mank, Gregory William, *The Hollywood Hissables*, Metuchen, NJ, Scarecrow Press, 1989

Mank, Gregory William, *Karloff and Lugosi: A Haunting Collaboration*, Jefferson, NC and London, McFarland & Co., Inc., 1990

Moore, Clayton, *I Was That Masked Man*, Dallas, Taylor Publishing Co., 1996

Peary, Danny, editor, *Close Ups (The Movie Star Book); Intimate Profiles by their Co-Stars, Directors, Screenwriters and Friends*, New York, Whitman Publishing, 1978

Pitts, Michael R., *Poverty Row Studios, 1929-1940, An Illustrated History of 53 Independent Film Companies*, Jefferson City, NC, and London, McFarland & Co., Inc., 1997

Pitts, Michael R., *Western Movies: A TV & Video Guide to 4,200 Genre Films*, Jefferson, NC, and London, McFarland & Co., Inc., 1986

Price, Michael H., *Hollywood Horrors*, Irvington, NJ, Shel-Tone Publications, 1993

Rainey, Dr. Bill G. "Buck," *The Life and Films of Buck Jones, The Sound Era*, Waynesville, NC, The World of Yesterday, 1991

Rainey, Dr. Bill G. "Buck," *Serials and Series: A World Filmography, 1912-1956*, Jefferson, NC, and London, McFarland & Co., Inc., 1999

Rhodes, Gary D., *Lugosi: His Life in Films, on Stage, and in the Hearts of Horror Lovers*, Jefferson City, NC, and London, McFarland & Co., Inc., 1997

Rickenbacker, Edward, V., *Rickenbacker: An Autobiography*, NJ, Prentiss-Hall, Inc., 1967

Rovin, Jeff, *The Return of the Wolf Man*, New York, Berkeley Boulevard Books, 1998

Senn, Bryan, *Golden Horrors: An Illustrated Critical Filmography of Terror Cinema, 1931-1939*, Jefferson City, NC, and London, McFarland & Co., Inc., 1996

Smith, Don G., *Lon Chaney, Jr.: Horror Film Star, 1906-1973*, Jefferson, NC, and London, McFarland & Co., Inc., 1996

Stedman, Raymond W., *The Serials: Suspense and Drama by Installment*, Norman, OK, University of Oklahoma Press, 1971/1977

Svehla, Gary and Susan Svehla, eds. *Midnight Marquee Actors Series: Bela Lugosi*, Baltimore, MD, Midnight Marquee Press, 1995

Svehla, Gary and Susan Svehla, eds. *Midnight Marquee Actors Series: Boris Karloff*, Baltimore, MD, Midnight Marquee Press, 1996

Svehla, Gary and Susan Svehla, eds. *Midnight Marquee Actors Series: Lon Chaney, Jr.,* Baltimore, MD, Midnight Marquee Press, 1997

Turner, George E., with Michael H. Price *et al.*, *The Cinema of Adventure, Romance & Terror*, Hollywood, CA, American Society of Cinematographers Press, 1989

Turner, George E., and Michael H. Price, *Forgotten Horrors: Early Talkie Chillers from Povery Row*, Cranbury, NJ, and London, A.S. Barnes & Co./The Tantivy Press, 1979

Turner, George E., and Michael H. Price, *Forgotten Horrors: Early Talkie Chillers from Povery Row*, Revised Edition, Forestville, CA, Eclipse Books, 1986

Turner, George E., and Michael H. Price, *Forgotten Horrors: The Definitive Edition*, Baltimore, MD, Midnight Marquee Press, 1999

Turner, George E., and Michael H. Price, *Human Monsters: The Bizarre Psychology of Movie Villains*, Northhampton, MA, Kitchen Sink Press, 1996

Tuska, Jon, *The Vanishing Legion: A History of Mascot Pictures, 1927-1935*, Jefferson, North Carolina and London, McFarland & Co. Inc., Inc., 1982

Witney, William, *In a Door, into a Fight, out a Door, into a Chase: Moviemaking Remembered by the Guy at the Door*, Jefferson, NC, and London, McFarland & Co., Inc., 1996

Zolotow, Maurice, *Shooting Star: A Biography of John Wayne*, New York, Simon & Schuster, 1974

Magazine Souces:

Collura, Joe, "The Three Musketeers' Desert Beauty," Waynesville, NC, *Cliffhanger*, No. 20, The World of Yesterday Publications, 1995

Everett, Eldon K., "Hollywood People... and Other Things: Serial Director of the 1930's, Ford Beebe," Muscatine, IA, *Classic Images*, No. 77, September, 1981

Geltzer, Elaine M. and George, "Ford Beebe" (Part Three), *Screen Facts*, No. 13, 1966

Hoffman, Eric, "Riders of Death Valley," *Serial World*, No. 33, 1982

Jackson, Charles Lee, "The Man Who Would Be Serial King," Evanston, IL, *Filmfax: The Magazine of Unusual Film and Television*, No. 20, May, 1990

Kohl, Leonard J., "The Sinister Serials of Bela Lugosi," Evanston, IL, *Filmfax: The Magazine of Unusual Film and Television*, No. 55, March/April, 1996

INDEX

**If you enjoyed this book
you will enjoy
Forgotten Horrors
by George E. Turner and
Michael H. Price.**

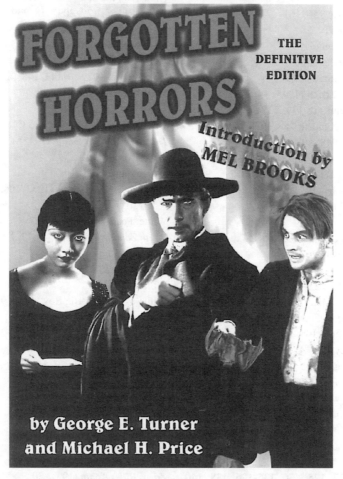

For more information or for a complete catalog of Midnight Marquee titles call 410-665-1198 or write to Midnight Marquee Press, Inc., 9721 Britinay Lane, Baltimore, MD 21234 or visit our website at www.Midmar.com.